Samuel Jo

INSU

Samuel Johnson's
INSULTS

A Compendium of
Snubs, Sneers, Slights, and Effronteries
from the Eighteenth-Century Master

Edited by **Jack Lynch**

LEVENGER
PRESS

WALKER & COMPANY
NEW YORK

First published in the United States of America in 2004 by
Walker Publishing Company Inc.
This paperback edition published by Walker in 2005

Distributed to the trade by Holtzbrinck Publishers

For information about permission to reproduce selections from this book, write to
Permissions, Walker & Company,
104 Fifth Avenue, New York, New York 10011.

The Library of Congress has cataloged the hardcover edition as follows:

Johnson, Samuel, 1709-1784.
Samuel Johnson's insults : a compendium of snubs, sneers, slights, and effronteries from
the eighteenth century master / edited by Jack Lynch.
p. cm.
Includes bibliographical references (p.) and index
ISBN: 0-8027-1428-5 (alk. paper)
1. Johnson, Samuel, 1709-1784—Quotations. 2. Invective—Quotations, maxims, etc.
3. Quotations, English. I. Lynch, Jack (John T.) II. Title.
PR3522.L94   2004
828'.609—dc22
2004049620

Paperback ISBN 0-8027-7732-5
ISBN 13 978-0-8027-7732-4

Book design by Maura Rosenthal/mspaceny

Illustrations by Susan Estelle Kwas

2 4 6 8 10 9 7 5 3 1

Visit Walker & Company's website at www.walkerbooks.com

Printed in the United States of America by RR Donnelley & Sons, Haddon Craftsman

to insult

- To treat with insolence or contempt.

- To trample upon; to triumph over.

from Samuel Johnson's *Dictionary of the English Language*

CONTENTS

Samuel Johnson's
INSULTS

INTRODUCTION

It is surely better a man should be abused than forgotten.
—Samuel Johnson

The Age of Johnson was an age of insults. Never has abuse been served up with more zest than in the eighteenth century.

It was the age of Jonathan Swift, the author of *Gulliver's Travels*, who once ridiculed an inelegant woman by saying, "She wears her clothes as if they had been thrown on by a pitchfork." It was the age of Alexander Pope, who in his mock-epic poem *The Dunciad* saw in one enemy only "a brain of feathers and a heart of lead." Across the English Channel, it was the age of Voltaire, whose passion for scolding the stupid landed him in prison for a year. "I have never made but one prayer to God," he said: "O Lord, make my enemies ridiculous. And God granted it."

Insolence and contempt were a favored mode of public discourse. Book reviews were often brutal hatchet jobs. Politics was rough-and-tumble, and it wasn't unusual to accuse an opponent of drunkenness, adultery, and worse. When the earl of Sandwich complained that his former friend, the libertine John Wilkes, "[would] die either on the gallows, or of the pox," Wilkes replied, "That must depend on whether I embrace your lordship's principles or your mistress." Caustic yellow journalism ruled. In a newspaper of the 1760s, Britain's secretary of the treasury, Samuel Martin, was called "the most treacherous, base, selfish, mean, abject, low-lived and dirty fellow, that ever *wriggled* himself into a secretaryship," and the article just got worse from there. We may find modern politics distasteful, but even the most negative campaigning to-day looks tame beside the average eighteenth-century parliamentary election.

◆ ◆ ◆

In this world where insults flew fast and furious, Samuel Johnson was second to none. He was born in 1709, when Pope and Swift were per-fecting their style, and even as a child he was known for his sharp tongue. During his brief stay at Oxford University in 1728 he amazed fellow students with the witty insolence he directed at his tutor. By the 1750s he was famous across England as the master of the put-down, as everyone who met him discovered. In her diaries Frances Burney— novelist, playwright, and one of Johnson's most talented young friends—called him "Mr. Turbulent," noting that "the freedom with which Dr Johnson condemns whatever he disapproves is astonishing." Another friend described the "roughness in his manner which subdued the saucy & terrified the Meek." This legendary "roughness" prompted Jon Winokur, the author of *The Portable Curmudgeon*, to include him in a list of "World-Class Curmudgeons." He's in distinguished company, alongside the likes of Ambrose Bierce, Groucho Marx, H. L. Mencken, George Bernard Shaw, Mark Twain, and Oscar Wilde.

Johnson achieved this status because he adored a good argument and relished verbal combat. As he told Sir John Hawkins, his longtime friend and first biographer, "I dogmatise and am contradicted, and in this conflict of opinions and sentiments I find delight." Few ever took more delight in conflict. When he recalled one night's discussion, he told James Boswell, another friend and even more famous biographer, "Well, we had good talk." Boswell reminded him of what he really enjoyed: "Yes, Sir; you tossed and gored several persons."

His fame made him the target of innumerable attacks, but Johnson never shrank from abuse—verbal assaults only energized him. As he once said of a writer who didn't respond well to criticism, "I hate a fellow whom pride, or cowardice, or laziness drives into a corner, and who does nothing when he is there but sit and *growl;* let him come out as I do, and *bark.*" After all, how much real harm can an insult do? When another of Johnson's friends, the scholar Elizabeth Carter, called one writer "a bad man" because "he used to talk uncharitably," Johnson ridiculed her. "Poh! poh! Madam; who is the worse for being talked of uncharitably?"

Hester Thrale, perhaps his closest friend, tells us he actually *liked* being the subject of uncharitable talk, on the no-publicity-is-bad-publicity principle. When Johnson was warned that one of his pamphlets was about to receive some harsh reviews, he replied, "Why now, these fellows are only advertising my book; it is surely better a man should be abused than forgotten." As he put it another time, "Abuse is often of service: there is nothing so dangerous to an author as silence; his name, like a shuttlecock, must be beat backward and forward, or it falls to the ground."

He loved this back-and-forth so much that he complained when he didn't make enough enemies. One of his most biting works, *Taxation No Tyranny,* was a fierce attack on the American colonists that infuriated patriots from Boston to Virginia. Their anger wasn't enough, though, for this staunchly royalist Englishman. "I think I have not been attacked enough for it," he mused. "Attack is the re-action; I never think I have hit hard, unless it rebounds."

If ever it seemed he was about to lose an argument, Johnson wasn't above cheating—or, as Boswell put it, "he had recourse to some sudden mode of robust sophistry." He loved "the sport of conversation" so much that he'd make perverse arguments just for the fun of it. Sometimes he didn't even care which side of an argument he took, as long as he got to argue. Once, for instance, he began, "Why, Sir, as to the good or evil of card-playing—." His friend David Garrick cut him off and announced to the crowd, "Now he is thinking which side he shall take." Whichever side he took, there was no escaping. The writer Oliver Goldsmith knew Johnson's mode well: "There is no arguing with Johnson," he said, "for if his pistol misses fire, he knocks you down with the butt end of it."

◆ ◆ ◆

This book collects some of Johnson's more devastating and entertaining insults, and gives us a vivid portrait of Johnson the Grouch, Johnson the Grump, Johnson the Curmudgeon. But it's only a partial picture. Occasionally, he could be genuinely mean-spirited, because he had a fearsome temper. Boswell compared him to "a warm West-Indian climate, where you have a bright sun, quick vegetation, luxuriant foliage, luscious fruits; but where the same heat sometimes produces thunder, lightning, and earthquakes, in a terrible degreee." When Johnson and Bishop Thomas Percy argued, for example, that temper flared until Percy accused him of rudeness. "Hold, Sir!" said Johnson. "Don't talk of rudeness. . . . We have done with civility. We are to be as rude as we please." Percy tried to patch things up: "Sir, I did not mean to be uncivil." "I cannot say so, Sir," retorted Johnson, "for I *did* mean to be uncivil." Likewise, after he taunted the writer Thomas Sheridan, he explained, "This, you see, was wanton and insolent; but I *meant* to be wanton and insolent."

Usually, though, Johnson didn't mean to be wanton and insolent. Most of his snubs arose not from anger but from his boundless wit and energy, for his sense of humor was prodigious. An entry in Boswell's diary describes a typical night's conversation in just two words: "Much laughing." Johnson, said David Garrick, "gives you a forcible hug, and shakes laughter out of you, whether you will or no." Johnson's own laugh, Boswell recorded, "was as remarkable as any circumstance in his manner. It was a kind of good humoured growl." Hester Thrale found that laugh "irresistible," as did his friend Tom Davies, who said, "He laughs like a rhinoceros."

♦ ♦ ♦

This collection is structured around Johnson's great *Dictionary of the English Language*, which first appeared in two large volumes in 1755. In my introduction to *Samuel Johnson's Dictionary: Selections from the 1755 Work That Defined the English Language*, I maintained that the *Dictionary* was mostly "a sober and modest affair." It certainly is that—and yet, whenever readers flip through the book, they always gravitate toward words like *blunderhead*, *fopdoodle*, and *pickleherring*. This little book lets us revel unashamedly in those eccentric and amusing entries. I've made a selection of the vocabulary of abuse from *abbey-lubber* to *zany*, along with some of Johnson's definitions and a few of the quotations he took from writers such as Swift, Pope, and especially Shakespeare to illustrate the way the words were used.

Stirred in with many of these *Dictionary* entries are anecdotes from

Johnson's own writings and conversation that show his own mastery of the barb. Some are well documented, although the authenticity of the spoken word is always questionable in the days before sound recording. Boswell, for instance—Johnson's most diligent biographer and memoirist—wrote down tens of thousands of words of his hero's conversation in his *Life of Samuel Johnson,* but who knows how accurate he was? And if Boswell is a questionable source, worse still are the many books of quotations assembled by people who never even knew Johnson.

Consider one jab that appears in many collections. Boswell was the target: He had drunk too much, as he often did, and Johnson berated him for it. In his defense, Boswell resorted to the old cliché *in vino veritas,* "there's truth in wine"—on this much, all the tale-tellers agree. But how exactly Johnson responded is unclear. Here's how Boswell himself reports on Johnson's reply: "Why, Sir, that may be an argument for drinking, if you suppose men in general to be liars. But, Sir, I would not keep company with a fellow, who lyes as long as he is sober, and whom you must make drunk before you can get a word of truth out of him." Hester Thrale, though, recalls a less philosophical and more pointed comeback: "That would be useless to a man who knew he was not a liar when he was sober." And according to another writer, Archibald Campbell, Johnson was pithier still: "What then unless a man has lived a lye?" What to do with these? At a distance of two and a half centuries, when there are multiple versions of a story, it's impossible to know exactly what Johnson said. In instances like this I've picked the one that seemed the best story to illustrate Johnson's quick and incisive wit.

In fact, Johnson may never have said some of the things attributed to him, and even the usually meticulous Boswell made mistakes. One famous line he attributed to Johnson wasn't Johnson's at all. When "a fellow . . . attacked him with some coarse raillery," Johnson supposedly fired back: "Sir, your wife, *under pretence of keeping a bawdy-house*, is a receiver of stolen goods." It's a fine line, but it's not Johnson's, since it appeared in a joke book published before Boswell was born. Like other masters of the quip—think of Abraham Lincoln, Mark Twain, and Winston Churchill—Johnson had countless quotations foisted upon him that he never spoke. For example: "Sir, your book is both good and original. Unfortunately the parts that are good are not original, and the parts that are original are not good." This one can't, alas, be found in any work by Johnson or his contemporaries. We often hear that Johnson defined *fishing* as "a stick and a string, with a worm at one end and a fool at the other." But this wasn't recorded until 1859, long after Johnson's death in 1784, and the same joke had been attributed to Jonathan Swift forty years earlier (though it probably wasn't Swift's, either). These quotations had probably circulated as "anonymous" until someone felt the need for an author; Johnson was there, and he served. On matters like this I've been careful to include only those stories that circulated during Johnson's lifetime or among those who knew him personally, and to take quotations of Johnson's directly from the original sources, with the spelling and punctuation unchanged.

The *Dictionary* entries are abridged, limited to those definitions and quotations that best illustrate the word's insulting nature. But each entry follows the logic and sequence of the original. First came the "headword," the word being defined, with the accented syllable marked. Words not yet naturalized as entirely English, such as *borachio* and *fico*, Johnson presented in italics. Then he usually gave an etymology, which appeared in brackets, tracing the word to its root. Some words got usage notes, as when he called them "cant" or jargon; sometimes he passed judgment, as when he called words that he considered unfit for dignified use "low" or "bad." Then came the definitions. Most but not all of the etymologies and definitions were his own; when they were borrowed, he wrote "Dict." to indicate the entry came from some other dictionary, or he cited his sources by name: Robert Ainsworth, Thomas Carew, Sir Thomas Hanmer, Stephen Skinner, and Francis Junius were all scholars and lexicographers who provided him with information. After the definitions came the quotations from illustrious authors, along with their names.

◆ ◆ ◆

In the preface to his *Dictionary*, Johnson regretted that the short quotations he took from Shakespeare and other writers wouldn't do justice to their authors: "It may sometimes happen, by hasty detruncation, that the general tendency of the sentence may be changed: the divine may desert his tenets, or the philosopher his system." I've felt exactly the same misgivings. In presenting only Johnson's grumpy side, I worry that readers may come away with a distorted image of Johnson as a bitter and crabby killjoy. Those who knew him knew better. "All he said was rough," Hester Thrale explained, but "all he did was gentle."

And yet, if a book of insults isn't an entirely fair portrait of the great lexicographer, Johnson's own fabled sense of humor should encourage us to approach his more devastating comments with a comparable sense of fun (even if Johnson dismissed *fun* in his *Dictionary* as "a low cant word"). And if the insults prompt readers to seek out a more accurate and complete picture of Johnson by reading his works or one of his many biographies, so much the better. Better, too, that he should be abused than forgotten.

THE INSULTS

A

ábbey-lubber A slothful loiterer in a religious house, under pretence of retirement and austerity.

> *This is no Father Dominic, no huge overgrown abbeylubber; this is but a diminutive sucking friar.* Dryd. Sp. Fr.

áirling [from *air*, for *gayety*.] A young, light, thoughtless, gay person.

árrant [a word of uncertain etymology, but probably from *errant*, which being at first applied to its proper signification to vagabonds, as an errant or arrant rogue, that is, a rambling rogue, lost, in time, its original signification, and being by its use understood to imply something bad, was applied at large to any thing that was mentioned with hatred or contempt.] Bad in a high degree.

> *A vain fool grows forty times an arranter sot than before.* L'Estrange's Fables.

❧Etymology wasn't Johnson's forte, but he was right on this one: *arrant* comes from *errant,* "wandering." It became part of the phrase *thief arrant* in the fourteenth century, and by the end of the sixteenth century it meant "anyone wicked."❧

ásshead [from *ass* and *head.*] One slow of apprehension; a blockhead.

B

báckbiter [from *backbite.*] A privy calumniator; a censurer of the absent.

báckfriend [from *back* and *friend.*] A friend backwards; that is, an enemy in secret.

❧After Johnson's death, many of his friends wrote biographies and memoirs—James Boswell's *Life of Samuel Johnson* was only the most famous book in a substantial library. All his biographers tried to show that they were Johnson's closest friend by filling their books with digs at their rivals. Boswell was especially jealous of Hester Thrale—Johnson spent more time with her than with him, and her *Anecdotes of Johnson* came out before his *Life*—so he loaded his biography with Johnson's private jabs at her. She was stung by the stories, "laughing & crying by turns for two Days," she wrote in her diary. "If Johnson was to me the back Friend he has represented—let it cure me of ever making *Friendship* more with any human Being!"❧

bággage [from *bag, bagage,* Fr.]

- The furniture and utensils of an army.

- A worthless woman; in French *bagaste;* so called, because such women follow camps.

❦ Like *hussy, baggage* was "often used ludicrously in slight disapprobation." When his young friend, the novelist and playwright Frances Burney, didn't come out to greet him right away, Johnson "half drolly and half reproachfully called out, 'Ah, you little baggage, you! and have you known how long I have been here, and never to come to me?'"❧

barbárian [*barbarus,* Lat. It seems to have signified at first only *foreign,* or a *foreigner;* but, in time, implied some degree of wildness or cruelty.]

- A brutal monster; a man without pity: a term of reproach.

- A man uncivilized; untaught; a savage.

Proud Greece, all nations else barbarians held,
Boasting, her learning all the world excell'd. Denham.

There were not different gods among the Greeks and barbarians.
Stillingfleet's Defence of Disc. on Romish Idolatry.

❦ The Latin *barbarus* comes from the Greek βαρβαρος, which means "anyone who doesn't speak Greek." To Greek ears, foreign speakers seemed to be making nonsense sounds—*bar bar bar bar.* From "foreign" it shifted to "uncivilized," and from there to "savage."❧

barber-monger A word of reproach in Shakespeare, which seems to signify a fop; a man decked out by his barber.

Draw, you rogue; for though it be night, the moonshines; I'll make a sop
of the moonshine of you; you whoreson, cullionly, barber-monger, draw.
Shakesp. King Lear.

bárrel-bellied [from *barrel* and *belly.*]
Having a large belly.

bawd [*baude*, old Fr.] A procurer, or pro-
curess; one that introduces men and
women to each other, for the promotion
of debauchery.

> *If your worship will take order for the*
> *drabs and the knaves, you need not to fear*
> *the bawds.* Shakesp. Measure for Meas.

bárrel-bellied

bédlam [corrupted from *Bethlehem*, the name of a religious house in
London, converted afterwards into an hospital for the mad and
lunatick.]

- A madhouse; a place appointed for the cure of lunacy.

- A madman; a lunatick.

Bedlam is named for a London convent, the Priory of St. Mary
Bethlehem, which by the fourteenth century served as a hospital for
the insane. It eventually gave a clipped form of its name, *bedlam*, to
the kind of chaos found in a "madhouse." After the hospital began al-
lowing visitors in the seventeenth century, it became a popular
tourist attraction. Johnson and Boswell paid a visit in 1775 and
found "the general contemplation of insanity was very affecting."

bédpresser [from *bed* and *press*.] A heavy lazy fellow.

This sanguine coward, this bedpresser, this horseback-breaker, this huge hill of flesh. Shakesp. Henry IV. p. i.

béllygod [from *belly* and *god*.] A glutton; one who makes a god of his belly.

❦Johnson wasn't fat, but he could be something of a bellygod himself. "Some people have a foolish way of not minding, or pretending not to mind, what they eat," he said. "For my part, I mind my belly very studiously." His belly would tell him whether things were right in a household: "Wherever the dinner is ill got," he said, "the family is somehow grossly wrong." One particularly rotten dinner at a nobleman's house prompted him to say of the cook, "I'd throw such a rascal into the river." On another occasion some bad roast mutton put him into a foul mood, and he rebuked the waiter: "It is as bad as bad can be: it is ill-fed, ill-killed, ill-kept, and ill-drest." He was always disappointed if his host served him "a plain dinner." Boswell heard him say, "This was a good dinner enough, to be sure; but it was not a dinner to *ask* a man to." Even a good meal could prompt rudeness. When Hester Thrale served Johnson some peas and praised them as "charming," Johnson grunted, "Perhaps they would be so—to a *pig*."❦

belswágger A cant word for a whoremaster.

bíter [from *bite*.] A tricker; a deceiver.

A biter is one who tells you a thing, you have no reason to disbelieve in itself, and perhaps has given you, before he bit you, no reason to disbelieve

it for his saying it; and, if you give him credit, laughs in your face, and
triumphs that he has deceived you. He is one who thinks you a fool,
because you do not think him a knave. Spectator, N° 504.

blab [from the verb.] A teltale; a thoughtless babbler; a treacherous
betrayer of secrets.

bláck-guard [from *black* and *guard*.] A cant word amongst the vulgar;
by which is implied a dirty fellow; of the meanest kind.

Let a black-guard boy be always about the house, to send on your
errands, and go to market for you on rainy days. Swift.

blóckhead [from *block* and *head*.] A stupid fellow; a dolt; a man without parts.

A blockhead rubs his thoughtless skull,
And thanks his stars he was not born a fool. Pope.

❧ How Johnson loved this word! One of his most famous maxims is
"No man but a blockhead ever wrote, except for money." (Perhaps
he was a blockhead himself, since he wrote hundreds of pages as fa-
vors to friends.) When "a very stupid maid" misunderstood a spoken message, he burst out angrily, "Blockhead, I'll write." Boswell
was struck by this: "I never heard the word *blockhead* applied to a
woman before, though I do not see why it should not."

At times his contempt for blockheads could turn physical. Early
in his career he worked with another writer, Tom Osborne, and the
two often argued. Osborne told people that Johnson, exasperated,
once whacked him over the head with a heavy folio. Johnson thought
Osborne was even more blockheaded for boasting about it. When

Hester Thrale asked him about it, he replied, "There is nothing to tell, dearest Lady, but that he was insolent and I beat him, and that he was a blockhead and told of it. . . . I have beat many a fellow, but the rest had the wit to hold their tongues."

blóckish [from *block*.] Stupid; dull.

blowze A ruddy fat-faced wench.

blúnderhead [from *blunder* and *head*.] A stupid fellow.

bóoby [a word of no certain etymology; Henshaw thinks it a corruption of *bull-beef* ridiculously; Skinner imagines it to be derived from *bobo*, foolish, Span. Junius finds *bowbard* to be an old Scottish word for a *coward*, a *contemptible fellow;* from which he naturally deduces *booby;* but the original of *bowbard* is not known.] A dull, heavy, stupid fellow; a lubber.

Of all the theories on the origin of the word *booby* that the etymologists Thomas Henshaw, Stephen Skinner, and Francis Junius offered, Skinner was probably right: the *Oxford English Dictionary* (*OED*) derives it from the Spanish *bobo*. Johnson attacked one Scottish minister as "the most ignorant booby and the grossest bastard," a passage Boswell wrote in his diary but excised from his published biography because it was too crude.

bóokworm [from *book* and *worm*.] A student too closely given to books; a reader without judgment.

Johnson had nothing against one minor bookworm, Thomas Edwards, whose *Canons of Criticism* scored some points against a major-league critic, William Warburton. But when someone suggested Edwards was just as good as Warburton, Johnson shut him up. "There is no proportion between the two men; they must not be named together. A fly, Sir, may sting a stately horse and make him wince; but one is but an insect, and the other is a horse still." ❧

boor [*beer*, Dutch; *gebure*, Sax.] A ploughman; a country fellow; a lout; a clown.

> *To one well-born, th' affront is worse and more,*
> *When he's abus'd and baffl'd by a boor.* Dryden.

boráchio [*borracho*, Span.] A drunkard.

> *How you stink of wine! D'ye think my niece will ever endure such a bora-chio! you're an absolute borachio.* Congreve's Way of the World.

❧ Shakespeare saw the attraction of the word and named a character Borachio in *Much Ado about Nothing*. ❧

bórrel [it is explained by Junius without etymology.] A mean fellow.

❧ The etymology is still uncertain, but the *OED* suspects it's from *borel*, "coarse clothing." Those who wore it would be called *borel* or *borrel*. ❧

brázenface [from *brazen* and *face*.] An impudent wretch.

búbbler [from *bubble*.] A cheat.

búffleheaded [from *buffle* and *head*.] A man with a large head, like a buffalo; dull; stupid; foolish.

buffóon [*buffon*, Fr.] A man whose profession is to make sport, by low jests and antick postures; a jackpudding.

❡ Among Johnson's favorite targets for good-humored insults were actors, whom he dismissed as talentless buffoons: "I look on them as no better than creatures set upon tables and joint-stools to make faces and produce laughter, like dancing dogs." "But, Sir," someone objected, "you will allow that some players are better than others?" "Yes, Sir," he said, "as some dogs dance better than others."

No actor was safe from his attacks. He took aim one day at Hannah Pritchard, who had starred in his own play, *Irene:* "It is wonderful," he said, "how little mind she had. Sir, she had never read the tragedy of Macbeth all through. She no more thought of the play out of which her part was taken, than a shoemaker thinks of the skin, out of which the piece of leather, of which he is making a pair of shoes, is cut." ❧

bull-calf [from *bull* and *calf.*] A he-calf; used for a stupid fellow: a term of reproach.

And, Falstaff, you carried your guts away as nimbly, and roared for mercy, and still ran and roared, as ever I heard bull-calf. Shakesp. Henry IV.

bull-head [from *bull* and *head.*] A stupid fellow; a blockhead.

búlly [Skinner derives this word from *burly*, as a corruption in the pronunciation; which is very probably right: or from *bulky*, or *bull-eyed;* which are less probable. May it not come from *bull*, the pope's letter, implying the insolence of those who came invested with authority from the papal court?] A noisy, blustering, quarrelling fellow: it is generally taken for a man that has only the appearance of courage.

> *'Tis so ridic'lous, but so true withal,*
> *A bully cannot sleep without a brawl.* Dryden's Juv. Sat. iii.

❦ The etymology is still unknown. *Bully* first appeared as a term of endearment in the sixteenth century and picked up negative associations only late in the seventeenth. ❧

búmpkin [This word is of uncertain etymology; Henshaw derives it from *pumpkin*, a kind of worthless gourd, or melon. This seems harsh. *Bump* is used amongst us for a knob, or lump; may not *bumpkin* be much the same with *clodpate, loggerhead, block,* and *blockhead.*] An awkward heavy rustick; a country lout.

> *A heavy bumpkin, taught with daily care,*
> *Can never dance three steps with a becoming air.* Dryden.

C

cáitiff [*cattivo,* Ital. a slave; whence it came to signify a bad man, with some implication of meanness; as *knave* in English, and *fur* in Latin; so certainly does slavery destroy virtue.

Ημισυ της αρετης αποαινυται δουλιον ημαρ. Homer.

A slave and a scoundrel are signified by the same words in many languages. A mean villain; a despicable knave.

Vile caitiff, vassal of dread and despair,
Unworthy of the common breathed air;
Why livest thou, dead dog, a longer day,
And dost not unto death thyself prepare? Fairy Queen, b. ii.

cállat, cállet A trull.

He call'd her whore; a beggar, in his drink,
Could not have laid such terms upon his callet. Shakesp.

cant [probably from *cantus*, Lat. implying the odd tone of voice used by vagrants; but imagined by some to be corrupted from *quaint.*]

- A corrupt dialect used by beggars and vagabonds.
- A particular form of speaking peculiar to some certain class or body of men.
- A whining pretension to goodness, in formal and affected terms.
- Barbarous jargon.

The affectation of some late authours, to introduce and multiply cant words, is the most ruinous corruption in any language. Swift.

❧ Empty words always bothered Johnson, who had too much respect for the language to use it laxly. Even little exaggerations could warrant a scolding. Boswell once said it would be "terrible" if Johnson were stuck in Harwich for a few days and unable to return home to London, but Johnson corrected him: "Don't, Sir, accustom yourself to use big words for little matters. It would *not* be *terrible*, though I *were* to be detained some time here." He famously advised Boswell, "Clear your *mind* of cant."

More serious canting could get him angry. In 1777, many feared a

French invasion, and all the talk was military. "Alas! alas!" cried John-son, "how this unmeaning stuff spoils all my comfort in my friends' conversation! Will the people never have done with it; and shall I never hear a sentence again without the *French* in it?"

Sometimes his attacks on canters could be harsh, even cruel. When Hester Thrale had news that a cousin had died in America, Johnson thought her sorrow was merely put on for the sake of ap-pearances: "Prithee, my dear, have done with canting; how would the world be the worse for it, I may ask, if all your relations were at once spitted like larks, and roasted for Presto's supper?" (Thrale explained, "Presto was the dog that lay under the table while we talked.")

But if false sorrow irritated him, false happiness infuriated him. Johnson wrote in his final days that he had lived "a life radically wretched," and his view of the world was surprisingly gloomy. He simply didn't believe other people who said they were happy. "It is all *cant*," he'd say, "the dog knows he is miserable all the time." "The world in its best state," he thought, "is nothing more than a larger assembly of beings, combining to counterfeit happiness which they do not feel." So when a friend told him his wife's sister was *really* happy, Johnson balked: "If your sister-in-law is really the contented being she professes herself Sir, her life gives the lie to every research of humanity; for she is happy without health, without beauty, with-out money, and without understanding. . . . I tell you, the woman is ugly, and sickly, and foolish, and poor; and would it not make a man hang himself to hear such a creature say, it was happy?"

cánter [from *cant.*] A term of reproach for hypocrites, who talk formally of religion, without obeying it.

Johnson, ever pious, found nothing funny in religious hypocrisy. Then again, he was so hard to work with that he often prompted people to take the Lord's name in vain. Although writing a dictionary single-handedly in nine years was a remarkable feat, he had gone six years past his deadline. One of his publishers, Andrew Millar, was glad to be finished with the long-overdue *Dictionary* and its feisty author: "Thank GOD I have done with him." Johnson, smiling, replied, "I am glad that he thanks GOD for any thing."

carle [*ceorl*, Saxon.] A mean, rude, rough, brutal man. We now use *churl*.

> *Answer, thou carle, and judge this riddle right,*
> *I'll frankly own thee for a cunning wight.* Gay's Pastorals.

> *The editor was a covetous carle, and would have his pearls of the*
> *highest price.* Bentley.

cárrion [*charogne*, Fr.]

- The carcase of something not proper for food.
- A name of reproach for a worthless woman.

churl [*ceorl*, Sax. *carl*, in German, is strong, rusticks being always observed to be strong bodied.]

- A rustick; a countryman; a labourer.
- A rude, surly, ill-bred man.

cit [contracted from *citizen*.] An inhabitant of a city, in an ill sense. A pert low townsman; a pragmatical trader.

We bring you now to show what different things,
The cits or clowns are from the courts of kings. Johnson.

Study your race, or the soil of your family will dwindle into cits or
squires, or run up into wits or madmen. Tatler.

❦The "ill sense" arises because city dwellers were usually trades-men rather than gentlemen; they had to *work* for their money, unlike those who simply *had* their money. The OED quotes Johnson's def-inition under *cit.*❧

clódpate [*clod* and *pate.*] A stupid fellow; a dolt; a thickscull.

clótpoll [from *clot* and *poll.*] Thickskull; blockhead.

concéitless [from *conceit.*] Stupid; without thought; dull of appre-hension.

Think'st thou, I am so shallow, so conceitless,
To be seduced by thy flattery. Shak. Two Gent. of Verona.

❦Johnson enjoyed skewering the empty-headed. On meeting "a dull tiresome fellow," he described him thus: "That fellow seems to me to possess but one idea, and that is a wrong one."❧

to cónycatch To catch a cony, is, in the old cant of thieves, to cheat; to bite; to trick.

I have matter in my head against you, and against your conycatching ras-
cals. Shakesp. Merry Wives of Windsor.

❦A *cony* is a rabbit. In eighteenth-century underworld slang, when a thief's "mark" was called a "cony," a thief was a "conycatcher."❧

cótquean [probably from *coquin*, French.] A man who busies himself with women's affairs.

❦ Hester Thrale's tongue could be as sharp as Johnson's. When she and Johnson had dinner with a boorish man, she described him as "particularly ugly, talking largely and loudly on every subject, understanding none as I could find, foppish without elegance, confident without knowledge, sarcastic without wit and old without experience, a man uniting every hateful quality, a deist, a dunce, and a cotquean." ❧

coxcómical [from *coxcomb*.] Foppish; conceited; a low word unworthy of use.

❦ Though a great supporter of the traditional English class structure, Johnson bristled around the idle rich. His friend Sir Joshua Reynolds, the greatest painter of the day, depended on them for patronage. Johnson once let out his opinion of the wealthy fops who posed for Reynolds's paintings: "If every man who wears a laced coat was extirpated, who would miss them?" Foppery, after all, "was never cured. . . . Once a coxcomb, and always a coxcomb." ❧

crábbed [from *crab*.]

- Harsh; unpleasing.
- Difficult; perplexing.
- Peevish; morose; cynical; sour.

> *O, she is*
> *Ten times more gentle, than her father's crabbed;*
> *And he's compos'd of harshness.* Shakespeare's Tempest.

❧ One of Johnson's harshest critics, the wealthy gadabout Horace Walpole, found Johnson's biography of Alexander Pope perplexing and peevish: "Dr. Johnson's *Life of Pope*," he wrote, "is a most trumpery performance, and stuffed with all his crabbed phrases and vulgarisms, and much trash as anecdotes." ❧

crack-brained [*crack* and *brained.*] Crazy; without right reason.

> *We have sent you an answer to the ill-grounded sophisms of those crack-brained fellows.* Arbuth. and Pope's Mart. Scrib.

crácker [from *crack.*] A noisy boasting fellow.

> *What cracker is this same that deafs our ears*
> *With this abundance of superfluous breath.* Shak. K. John.

❧ The satirist John Wolcot, known as "Peter Pindar," wrote a poem sniping at both Johnson's famous *Rambler* essays and his even more famous biographer, James Boswell:

> *Yes! whilst the* RAMBLER *shall a* COMET *blaze,*
> *And gild a world of darkness with his rays,*
> THEE *too, that* WORLD, *with wonderment, shall hail,*
> *A lively, bouncing* CRACKER *at his* TAIL! ❧

crack-hemp [*crack* and *hemp.*] A wretch fated to the gallows; a crack-rope. *Furcifer.*

> ❧ *Furcifer* is Latin for "rascal" or "someone bound for the gallows." ❧

crack-rope [from *crack* and *rope.*] A fellow that deserves hanging.

> ❧ When "a dull country magistrate" prattled on about his legal prowess and boasted of "having sentenced four convicts to trans-

portation" to the colonies to serve out a life sentence of exile, John-son couldn't bear the tiresome windbag any longer. "I heartily wish, Sir, that I were a fifth."

cúckoldmaker [*cuckold* and *make*.] One that makes a practice of cor-rupting wives.

In his annotated edition of Shakespeare's *Works*, Johnson noted that the Bard couldn't resist jokes about infidelity: "There is no im-age which our authour appears so fond of as that of a cuckold's horns. Scarcely a light character is introduced that does not endeav-our to produce merriment by some allusion to horned husbands."

cúdden, cúddy [without etymology.] A clown; a stupid rustick; a low dolt: a low bad word.

The slavering cudden, propp'd upon his staff,
Stood ready gaping with a grinning laugh. Dryden.

cúllion [*coglione*, a fool, Ital. perhaps from *scullion*. It seems to import meanness rather than folly.] A scoundrel; a mean wretch.

Up to the breach, you dogs; avaunt, you cullions. Shakes.

Cullion does indeed come from Italian *coglione*, but it has nothing to do with *scullion*: It's a vulgar Italian word for "testicles." Its earli-est uses in English mean the same thing; only later did it become a general term of abuse.

cúlly [*coglione*, Ital. a fool.] A man deceived or imposed upon; as, by sharpers or a strumpet.

cunctátor [Latin.] One given to delay; a lingerer; an idler; a sluggard.

cur [*korre*, Dutch.]

- A worthless degenerate dog.
- A term of reproach for a man.

D

dándiprat [*dandin*, French.] A little fellow; an urchin: a word used sometimes in fondness, sometimes in contempt.

dángler [from *dangle*.] A man that hangs about women only to waste time.

dápperling [from *dapper*.] A dwarf; a dandiprat. Ainsworth.

dástard [*adastriga*, Saxon.] A coward; a poltron; a man infamous for fear.

> Dastard and drunkard, mean and insolent;
> Tongue-valiant hero, vaunter of thy might,
> In threats the foremost, but the last in fight. Dryden.

débile [*debilis*, Lat.] Weak; feeble; languid; faint; without strength; imbecile; impotent.

disard [*disi disig*, Saxon, a fool, Skinner; *diseur*, French, Junius.] A prattler; a boasting talker. This word is inserted both by Skinner and Junius; but I do not remember it.

❦ *Disard* probably comes from the Old French *disour*, "speaker"; it meant "storyteller," and later "jester." At some point it was confused with *dizzy*. Johnson couldn't remember seeing the word except in the etymological dictionaries of Stephen Skinner and Francis Junius, but it appears in works by authors he had read, including John Skelton and Sir Thomas Elyot. ❦

ditch [*dic*, Saxon; *diik*, Erse.] Ditch is used, in composition, of any thing worthless, or thrown away into ditches.

Poor Tom, when the foul fiend rages, eats cowdung for sallets, swallows the old rat, and the ditch-dog. Shakespeare.

dógcheap [*dog* and *cheap*.] Cheap as dogs meat; cheap as the offal bought for dogs.

doghéarted [*dog* and *heart*.] Cruel; pitiless; malicious.

　　His unkindness,
That stript her from his benediction, turn'd her
To foreign casualties, gave her dear rights
To his doghearted daughters. Shakespeare's King Lear.

dog-trick [*dog* and *trick*.] An ill turn; surly or brutal treatment.

Learn better manners, or I shall serve you a dog-trick: come, down upon all four immediately; I'll make you know your rider. Dryden's Don Sebastian.

dolt [*dol* Teutonick.] A heavy stupid fellow; a blockhead; a thickscul; a loggerhead.

> *Thou hast not half that power to do me harm,*
> *As I have to be hurt: oh, gull! oh, dolt!*
> *As ignorant as dirt!* Shakespeare's Othello.

> *Like men condemn'd to thunder-bolts,*
> *Who, ere the blow, become mere dolts;*
> *They neither have the hearts to stay,*
> *Nor wit enough to run away.* Hudibras, p. iii. cant. 2.

doodle [a cant word, perhaps corrupted from *do little, Faineant.*] A trifler; an idler.

> ❊ *Doodle* does not come from *do little* (French *faineant*), but seems to be related to the German *Dudeltopf*: literally "a nightcap," figuratively "a simpleton." ❊

dotard [from *dote.*] A man whose age has impaired his intellects; a man in his second childhood; called in some provinces a *twichild*.

doxy A whore; a loose wench.

> ❊ Johnson liked the word and enjoyed teasing one of the nieces of the Shakespearean actor David Garrick by calling her Miss Doxy. ❊

drab [*drabbe*, Saxon, lees.] A whore; a strumpet.

> *If your worship will take order for the drabs and the knaves, you need not*
> *to fear the bawds.* Shakespeare.

> *Curs'd be the wretch so venal, and so vain,*
> *Paltry and proud as drabs in Drury-lane.* Pope.

❧ The adjective *drab*, meaning "dull-colored," doesn't appear in the *Dictionary*. It didn't enter the language until 1775, twenty years after the first edition was complete, and two years after Johnson's last revision of the book.☙

dráffy [from *draff*.] Worthless; dreggy.

drázel [perhaps corrupted from *drossel*, the scum or dross of human nature; or from *droslesse*, French, a whore.] A low, mean, worthless wretch.

droil [by Junius understood a contraction of *drivel*.] A drone; a sluggard.

dróssy [from *dross*.]

- Full of scorious or recrementitious parts; full of dross.
- Worthless; foul; feculent.

> *Your intention bold,*
> *As fire these drossy rhymes to purify,*
> *Or as elixir to change them into gold.* Donne.

drótchel [corrupted perhaps from *dretchel*. To dretch, in Chaucer, is to *idle*, to *delay*. *Droch*, in Frisick, is *delay*.] An idle wench; a sluggard. In Scottish it is still used.

❧ Johnson probably learned about words like this from his assistants, the six amanuenses, five of whom came from Scotland. Frisick (or Frisian) is a language still spoken in parts of the Netherlands and Germany, and is one of the closest cousins of English.☙

drudge [from the verb.] One employed in mean labour; a slave; one doomed to servile occupation.

❧ The great lexicographer could even accuse himself of drudgery: he defines *lexicographer* as "a writer of dictionaries; a harmless drudge." ❧

dúlhead [*dull* and *head*.] A blockheard; a wretch foolish and stupid; a dolt.

dull [*dwl*, Welsh; *dole*, Saxon; *dol*, mad, Dutch.] Stupid; doltish; blockish; unapprehensive; indocile; slow of understanding.

He that hath learned no wit by nature, nor art, may complain of gross breeding, or comes of a very dull kindred. Shak.

❧ Johnson, always oppressed by tedium, was forever on the lookout for things that could hold his attention. No crime, then, was worse than dullness; calling a writer *dull* amounted to a critical death sentence. Johnson used the term all the time, to devastating effect. His onetime friend Thomas Sheridan, for example, was "dull, naturally dull; but it must have taken him a great deal of pains to become what we now see him. Such an excess of stupidity, Sir, is not in Nature."

Some lively people were dull writers. The biographer Thomas Birch, for instance, was a fine talker but a boring author: "Tom Birch is as brisk as a bee in conversation; but no sooner does he take a pen in his hand, than it becomes a torpedo [electric eel] to him, and benumbs all his faculties."

Others were entertaining writers but dull people. At the top of this list was his friend Oliver Goldsmith, the author of *The Vicar of Wakefield* and *She Stoops to Conquer:* "No man was more foolish when he had not a pen in his hand, or more wise when he had." Johnson found it "amazing how little Goldsmith knows. He seldom comes where he is not more ignorant than any one else."

But some managed to be dull *everywhere.* Thomas Gray—remembered for his "Elegy Written in a Country Churchyard," one of the most famous poems in the English language—was "a dull fellow" all around. Boswell argued that Gray might have been dull company, but surely he wasn't dull in poetry? "Sir," Johnson returned, "he was dull in company, dull in his closet, dull everywhere. He was dull in a new way, and that made many people think him GREAT."

dunce [A word of uncertain etymology; perhaps from *dum,* the Dutch stupid.] A dullard; a dolt; a thickskul; a stupid indocile animal.

Dunce comes from John Duns Scotus, one of the most influential philosophers of the Middle Ages. He was widely read in the medieval universities, but the Renaissance brought a backlash against old-fashioned scholasticism. This led to a war of words between the advocates of the new learning and the more conservative Dunsmen, or Dunses. Soon any backward thinker could be labeled a *dunce.*

The eighteenth century delighted in castigating dunces. The classic attack is Alexander Pope's mock-epic poem *The Dunciad,* which appeared while Johnson was a student; it pretends to celebrate the dim-witted hack writers who worship the goddess Dulness. Growing weary of a conversation with a nearby dunce, Johnson thought back to the good old days when writers like Pope and Swift savaged such people mercilessly: "It was worth while being a dunce then. Ah, Sir, hadst *thou* lived in those days! It is not worth while being a dunce now, when there are no wits."

Dunce was one of Johnson's favorite terms of abuse, whether real or affectionate. To a friend who found Laurence Sterne's novel *Tristram*

Shandy very moving, he explained, "Why, that is, because, dearest, you're a dunce." But such matters require precision. When someone called a particular writer a *dunce*, he was swiftly corrected: "No, Sir," said Johnson. "The fellow is no dunce; but he is a *damned fool*." ❧

dúnghil Sprung from the dunghil; mean; low; base; vile; worthless.

dupe [*dupe*, French, from *duppe*, a foolish bird easily caught.] A credulous man; a man easily tricked.

❧ Johnson hated the thought of being anyone's dupe, and it made him a skeptic in all his dealings with others. He rarely fell for cheap tricks. When Lord Chesterfield tried to flatter him into dedicating the *Dictionary* to him (see the note on **patron**), Johnson didn't fall for it: "This courtly device failed of its effect," Boswell wrote. "Johnson, who thought that 'all was false and hollow,' despised the honeyed words, and was even indignant that Lord Chesterfield should, for a moment, imagine, that he could be the dupe of such an artifice." ❧

E

enthúsiast [ενθυσιαω.]

• One who vainly imagines a private revelation; one who has a vain confidence of his intercourse with God.

• One of a hot imagination, or violent passions.

❦ It's odd to think of *enthusiast* as an insult, but in Johnson's day it meant "someone mentally unbalanced." The Greek word means "filled with a god"; enthusiasts were religious fanatics who thought God spoke to them. Johnson thought the poet Milton, for instance, with his unconventional religious beliefs, was "no better than a wild enthusiast."

The word picked up its present meaning in Johnson's lifetime. When someone said he was "an *enthusiastical* farmer," Johnson was puzzled, and chuckled: "What can he do in farming by his *enthusiasm?*" But Boswell, a generation younger, knew what he meant: "He who wishes to be successful, or happy, ought to be enthusiastical, that is to say, very keen in all the occupations or diversions of life." ❦

erke [*earg*, Saxon.] Idle; lazy; slothful. An old word.

> For men therein should hem delite;
> And of that dede be not erke,
> But oft sithes haunt that werke. Chaucer.

evilwórker [*evil* and *work.*] One who does ill.

F

facinérious [corrupted by Shakespeare from *facinorous; facinus, facinoris,* Latin.] Wicked; facinorous.

'Tis strange, 'tis very strange, that is the brief and the tedious of it; and
he's of a most facinerious spirit that will not acknowledge it. Shakes.
All's well that ends well.

fáitour [*faitard*, French.] A scoundrel; a rascal; a mean fellow; a
poltron. An old word now obsolete.

Into new woes unweeting I was cast,
By this false faitour. Fairy Queen, b. i. cant. 4. stan. 47.

fátwitted [*fat* and *wit*.] Heavy; dull; stupid.

Thou art so fatwitted with drinking old sack, and unbuttoning thee after
supper, and sleeping upon benches in the afternoon, that thou hast forgotten. Shakes. Henry IV.

❦Sometimes Johnson grew impatient with the lesser wits that
flocked around him. Oliver Goldsmith once suggested that new
members should be added to the Literary Club, their famous "assembly of good fellows" formed in 1764, because "there can now be
nothing new among us: we have travelled over one another's minds."
Johnson became "a little angry," says Boswell, and retorted, "Sir, you
have not travelled over *my* mind, I promise you."❦

fávourite [*favori, favorite*, French; *favorita*, Ital.] One chosen as a com-
panion by his superiour; a mean wretch whose whole business is by
any means to please.

féculent [*faeculentus*, Lat. *feculent*, French.] Foul; dreggy; excre-
mentitious.

fico [Italian.] An act of contempt done with the fingers, expressing a *fig for you.*

to fig [See *fico*.] To insult with fico's or contemptuous motions of the fingers.

> *When Pistol lies, do this, and fig me like*
> *The bragging Spaniard.* Shakespeare's Henry IV.

⟐ In his notes on Shakespeare, Johnson explained this custom: "'To fig,' in Spanish, *Higas dar*, is to insult by putting the thumb between the fore and middle finger. From this Spanish custom we yet say in contempt, 'a fig for you.'" ⟐

fínical [from *fine*.] Nice; foppish; pretending to superfluous elegance.

flagítious [from *flagitius*, Latin.] Wicked; villainous; atrocious.

flásher [from *flash*.] A man of more appearance of wit than reality.

⟐ In 1779, Hester Thrale and Frances Burney joked about writing their own periodical paper, like Johnson's *Rambler* or *Idler*. Thrale recorded in her diary: "What says I shall we call our Paper? Oh the Flasher to be sure says She—we have a Hack Phrase here at Streatham of calling ev'ry thing *Flash* which we want other folks to call *Wit*." ⟐

to fleer [*fleardian*, to trifle, Saxon; *fleardan*, Scottish. Skinner thinks it formed from *leer*.]

- To mock; to gibe; to gest with insolence and contempt.

> *Dares the slave*
> *Come hither, cover'd with an antick face,*
> *To fleer and scorn at our solemnity.* Shak. Rom. and Juliet.

• To leer; to grin with an air of civility.

> *How popular and courteous; how they grin and fleer upon every man they*
> *meet!* Burton on Melancholy.

fléshmonger [from *flesh*.] One who deals in flesh; a pimp.

> *Was the duke a fleshmonger, a fool, and a coward, as you then reported*
> *him?* Shakespeare's Measure for Measure.

fon [Scott. A word now obsolete.] A fool; an ideot.

> *Sicker I hold him for a greater fon,*
> *That loves the thing he cannot purchase.* Spenser's Past.

fond [*fonn*, Scottish. A word of which I have found no satisfactory
etymology. To *fonne* is in Chaucer to doat, to be foolish.] Foolish; silly;
indiscreet; imprudent; injudicious.

> *Grant I may never prove so fond*
> *To trust man on his oath or bond.* Shakespeare's Timon.

❦ Johnson's guess at the etymology is probably right. *To fon* meant
"to act the fool," and someone who was foolish was *fonned.* ❧

fool [*ffol*, Welsh; *fol*, Islandick; *fol*, French.] One whom nature has
denied reason; a natural; an idiot.

> *Do'st thou call me fool, boy?*

—*All thy other titles thou hast given away; that thou wast born with.*
Shakespeare's King Lear.

footlicker [*foot* and *lick*.] A slave; an humble fawner; one who licks the foot.

fop [A word probably made by chance, and therefore without etymology.] A simpleton; a coxcomb; a man of small understanding and much ostentation; a pretender; a man fond of show, dress, and flutter; an impertinent.

❧ The origin is still unknown. *Fop* originally meant "fool" and later "a man fond of show, dress and flutter." The *OED* finds the first example of the sense "a conceited person; a pretender to wit" in a work from 1755, the year Johnson's *Dictionary* was published—but it was almost certainly around before that. ❧

fopdoodle [*fop* and *doodle*.] A fool; an insignificant wretch.

Where sturdy butchers broke your noodle,
And handled you like a fopdoodle. Hudibras, p. ii.

foutra [from *foutre*, French.] A fig; a scoff; an act of contempt.

A foutra for the world, and worldlings base. Shak. H. IV.

❧ Johnson decently skirts the meaning of the French *foutre*. The *New Cassell's French Dictionary* has this note: "Vulg. and not decent; generally written f. . . ." As one might guess, its meaning is the same as the English f. . . . ❧

fren A worthless woman. An old word wholly forgotten.

to Frénchify [from *French*.] To infect with the manner of France; to make a coxcomb.

❧ Making fun of the French has been the English national sport at least since 1066. Someone complimented Johnson on succeeding with his *Dictionary* where the French had failed. "Why, what would you expect, dear Sir," he said, "from fellows that eat frogs?" Commenting on the way the French were divided into aristocrats and peasants, with no middle class, he said, "The French, Sir, are a very silly People, they have no common life. Nothing but the two ends, Beggary and Nobility. . . . They are much behind-hand, stupid, ignorant creatures."

It wasn't just the French: Johnson enjoyed playing John Bull, the Englishman's Englishman, making fun of every other country on the globe. One friend noted that "his unjust contempt for foreigners was, indeed, extreme," and heard him quote Hugo Meynell: "*For any thing I see, foreigners are fools.*" But his friend the writer Hannah More insisted he wasn't really a bigot: "The prejudices he had to countries," she explained, "did not extend to individuals." ❧

fríbbler [from the verb.] A trifler.

A fribbler is one who professes rapture for the woman, and dreads her consent. Spectator, N° 288.

fub A plump chubby boy. Ainsworth.

fústian [*futaine*, French, from *fuste*, a tree, because cotton grows on trees.]

- A kind of cloth made of linen and cotton, and perhaps now of cotton only.

- A high swelling kind of writing made up of heterogeneous parts, or of words and ideas ill associated; bombast.

I am much deceived if this be not abominable fustian; that is, thoughts and words ill sorted, and without the least relation to each other.
Dryden's Spanish Fryar, Dedication.

❧ The popular Scottish poet James Thomson was renowned for his long, blank-verse poem *The Seasons*, and Johnson admitted he had some "true poetical genius." But Thomson could be a sloppy writer, simply throwing out "a cloud of words," Johnson complained, from which "the sense can hardly peep through." Once Johnson performed an experiment. He began reading aloud from *The Seasons*, and a friend praised Thomson extravagantly. Johnson then revealed his secret: "Sir, I have omitted every other line."

fústilarian [from *fusty*.] A low fellow; a stinkard; a scoundrel. A word used by Shakespeare only.

Away, you scullion, you rampallian, you fustilarian: I'll tickle your catastrophe. Shakespeare's Henry IV. p. ii.

G

garlickeáter [*garlick* and *eat*.] A mean fellow.
     You've made good work,
  You and your apron men, that stood so much

Upon the voice of occupation, and
The breath of garlickeaters. Shakespeare's *Coriolanus*.

❧ In his notes on Shakespeare's *Coriolanus*, Johnson explains the origin of the word: "To smell of garlick was once such a brand of vulgarity, that garlick was a food forbidden to an ancient order of Spanish knights." Jonathan Swift seems to have shared Shakespeare's distaste: He admitted the archbishop of Dublin was "a wit and a scholar," but still insisted, "I hate him as I hate garlick." ❧

giddybrained [*giddy* and *brain*.] Careless; thoughtless.

❧ Johnson must have liked the word: Lady Giddy is a character in his essay *Rambler* No. 55. But he insisted to Hester Thrale that he and Thrale's young daughter Queeney "are both steady, and may be trusted; we are none of the giddy gabblers, we think before we speak." ❧

giglet [*geagl*, Saxon; *geyl*, Dutch; *gillet*, Scottish, is still retained.] A wanton; a lascivious girl. Now out of use.

　　Young Talbot was not born
To be the pillage of a giglet wench. Shakesp.
　　Henry VI.

glassgazing [*glass* and *gazing*.] Finical; often contemplating himself in a mirrour.

A whorson, glassgazing, superserviceable, finical rogue. Shakespeare's *King Lear*.

glike [*glig*, Saxon.] A sneer; a scoff; a flout. Not now in use.

glássgazing

to gloze [*glesan*, Saxon.] To flatter; to wheedle; to insinuate; to fawn.

Man will hearken to his glozing lies,
And easily transgress. Milton's Paradise Lost, b. iii.

❦ Though he savored a well-placed compliment, Johnson found too much flattery cloying. Hester Thrale recalls the time "a literary dame" spent a whole day in complimenting Johnson with "coarse and incessant flattery." Finally, he had enough. He put her in her place, telling her to "consider what her flattery was worth before she choaked *him* with it." ❧

górbelly [from *gor*, dung, and *belly*, according to Skinner and Junius. It may perhaps come from *gor*, Welsh, beyond, too much; or, as seems to me more likely, may be contracted from *gormand*, or *gormand's belly*, the belly of a glutton.] A big paunch; a swelling belly. A term of reproach for a fat man.

❦ According to the *OED*, Skinner and Junius were right. ❧

górmand [*gourmand*, French.] A greedy eater; a ravenous luxurious feeder.

grammaticáster [Latin.] A mean verbal pedant; a low grammarian.

❦ Johnson could be a harsh grammarian himself. He noted of the dedication to James Harris's treatise on language, *Hermes*, "though but fourteen lines long, there were six grammatical faults in it." Harris came in for plenty of Johnsonian abuse: Although he was "a sound sullen scholar," Johnson added that he "however is a prig, and a bad prig. I looked into his book, and thought he did not understand his own system." ❧

grúmbler [from *grumble*.] One that grumbles; a murmurer; a discontented man.

❧ Johnson sometimes facetiously referred to himself as "Mr. Grumbler," especially when his health was bad. "It is so *very* difficult for a sick man not to be a scoundrel," he told Hester Thrale. "Oh! set the pillows soft, here is Mr. Grumbler o'coming: Ah! let no air in for the world, Mr. Grumbler will be here presently."

But for heaven's sake don't bore him with complaints about your own health. To a friend "who lamented the tender state of his *inside*," he said, "Do not be like the spider, man; and spin conversation thus incessantly out of thy own bowels." ❧

H

to hag [from the noun.] To torment; to harrass with vain terrour.

How are superstitious men hagged out of their wits with the fancy of omens, tales, and visions! L'Estrange.

half-blooded [*half* and *blood*.] Mean; degenerate.

half-scholar Imperfectly learned.

We have many half-scholars now-a-days, and there is much confusion and inconsistency in the notions and opinions of some persons. Watts's Improvement of the Mind.

❦ Johnson, always aware of Alexander Pope's maxim that "a little learning is a dangerous thing," was impatient with intellectual dilettantes. When the actor Samuel Foote said that Johnson had to admit that the Scots were well educated, Johnson corrected him: "You are very much mistaken upon that point. I grant you they have all a *mouthful* of learning, but not one of them a *bellyful*." ❧

half-wit [*half* and *wit*.] A blockhead; a foolish fellow.

Half-wits are fleas, so little and so light,
We scarce could know they live, but that they bite. Dryden.

hedge, prefixed to any word, notes something mean, vile, of the lowest class: perhaps from a *hedge,* or *hedge-born man,* a man without any known place of birth.

There are five in the first shew: the pedant, the braggart, the hedge-priest, the fool, and the boy. Shakespeare.

The clergy do much better than a little hedge, contemptible, illiterate vicar can be presumed to do. Swift.

hell-kite [*hell* and *kite*.] Kite of infernal breed. The term *hell* prefixed to any word notes detestation.

All my pretty ones?
Did you say all? What, all? Oh, hell-kite! all?
What, all my pretty chickens, and their dam,
At one fell swoop? Shakesp. Macbeth.

high-viced Enormously wicked.

hílding [*hild*, Saxon, signifies a lord: perhaps *hilding* means originally a little lord in contempt, for a man that has only the delicacy or bad qualities of high rank; or a term of reproach abbreviated from *hinderling*, degenerate. Hughes's Spens.]

- A sorry, paltry, cowardly fellow.

He was some hilding fellow, that had stol'n
The horse he rode on. Shakespeare's Henry IV. p. i.

- It is used likewise for a mean woman.

Laura, to his lady, was but a kitchen wench;
Helen and Hero, hildings and harlots. Shak. Rom. and Jul.

❧ The origin of *hilding* is still unknown. The *OED* guesses it might come from *hield*, "to bend down." Johnson took many obsolete words from the glossary that the scholar John Hughes added to his edition of Edmund Spenser's poems in 1715. ❧

hínderling [from *hind* or *hinder*.] A paltry, worthless, degenerate animal.

hóiden [*hoeden*, Welsh; *foemina levioris famae*, Latin.] An ill-taught awkward country girl.

❧ The etymology remains obscure. When *hoiden* was first used at the end of the sixteenth century, it referred to men; it began to be applied strictly to women at the end of the seventeenth century. ❧

hotbráined [*hot* and *brain.*] Violent; vehement; furious.

huff [from *hove*, or *hoven*, swelled: he is *huffed up* by distempers. So in some provinces we still say the bread *huffs up*, when it begins to *heave* or ferment: *huff*, therefore, may be ferment. To be in a *huff* is then to be in a *ferment*, as we now speak.] A wretch swelled with a false opinion of his own value.

hotbráined

> As for you, colonel *huff-cap*, we shall try before a civil magistrate who's the greater plotter. Dryden's Spanish Fryar.

> ⅏ Often Johnson would grow exasperated with a sparring partner who thought too highly of himself. When, in the midst of a dispute, one opponent said, "I don't understand you, Sir," Johnson rejoined, "Sir, I have found you an argument; but I am not obliged to find you an understanding." ⅏

hunks [*hunskur*, sordid, Islandick.] A covetous sordid wretch; a miser; a curmudgeon.

> *The old hunks was well served, to be tricked out of a whole hog for the securing of his puddings.* L'Estrange.

hússy [corrupted from *housewife*: taken in an ill sense.] A sorry or bad woman; a worthless wench. It is often used ludicrously in slight disapprobation.

> ⅏ Hussy was just a synonym for housewife beginning in 1530. It picked up its negative connotations around 1650. ⅏

I

idiot [*idiote*, Fr. *idiota*, Latin; ιδιωτης.] A fool; a natural; a changeling; one without the powers of reason.

> *Life is a tale,*
> *Told by an idiot, full of sound and fury,*
> *Signifying nothing.* Shakespeare's Macbeth.

❦ The Greek ιδιωτης, *idiotes*, means "a private man; a loner." From there it came to mean "a layman; unlearned," then moved to "ignorant," and finally to "stupid." ❧

idler [from *idle*.] A lazy person; a sluggard.

> *Thou sluggish idler, dilatory slave.* Irene.

❦ It's hard to believe, but Johnson thought of himself as a lazy person and a sluggard. His friends marveled at how someone who single-handedly wrote a dictionary, edited the complete plays of Shakespeare, and wrote three hundred essays and more than fifty biographies could think himself unproductive, but Johnson's standards were high. It's clearest in the title of his last series of essays: after *The Rambler* and *The Adventurer* came *The Idler.* It's also telling that the quotation he used (above) comes from his own play, *Irene.* ❧

inconvérsable [*in* and *conversable*.] Incommunicative; ill qualified by temper for conversation; unsocial.

❦ Johnson made up his own word to show how important sociability was to him: Sir John Hawkins, he said, "is a very *unclubable* man." ❧

interméddler [from *intermeddle.*] One that interposes officiously; one that thrusts himself into business to which he has no right.

jábberer [from *jabber.*] One who talks inarticulately or unintelligibly.

> *Out cant the Babylonian labourers*
> *At all their dialects of jabberers.* Hudibras, p. iii.

jack [Probably by mistake from *Jaques,* which in French is *James.*] The diminutive of *John.* Used as a general term of contempt for saucy or paltry fellows.

> *I have in my mind*
> *A thousand raw tricks of these bragging Jacks,*
> *Which I will practise.* Shakes. Merchant of Venice.

❦ Beginning in the middle of the sixteenth century, *Jack* stood for any common man, like "Tom, Dick, and Harry." As this common man became ever more common, says the *OED,* the word came to refer especially to "a low-bred or ill-mannered fellow." ❧

jackalént [*Jack in Lent,* a poor starven fellow.] A simple sheepish fellow.

jack pudding [*jack* and *pudding.*] A zani; a merry Andrew.

A buffoon is called by every nation by the name of the dish they like best: in French jean pottage, and in English jack pudding. Guardian.

❦ For Johnson, most actors were no better than jack puddings. Boswell tried to explain his mysterious "prejudice against play-ers": he attributed it to "first, the imperfection of his organs" (Johnson was nearly blind and deaf); "secondly, the cold rejection of his tragedy" (no theater wanted to produce his play, *Irene*); and "lastly, the brilliant success of Garrick." David Garrick was John-son's old friend and former student, and the two came to London together in 1737. But while Johnson labored in obscurity, Garrick quickly became the most famous actor in Europe. Johnson there-fore relished every opportunity to tear him down. When asked for his opinion of one of Garrick's poems, he said he couldn't bear to read it: "I got through half a dozen lines, but I could observe no other subject than eternal dulness. I don't know what is the mat-ter with David." And when Boswell tried to defend Garrick, John-son retorted, "The next subject you talk to him of, 'tis two to one he is wrong."

But heaven help anyone *else* who presumed to ridicule Garrick. A friend observed that "when anybody else did so, he fought for the dog like a tiger." And Sir Joshua Reynolds once said that "Johnson considered Garrick to be as it were his *property*. He would allow no man either to blame or to praise Garrick in his presence, without contradicting him." ❧

jade [The etymology of this word is doubtful: Skinner derives it from *gaad*, a goad, or spur.]

- A horse of no spirit; a hired horse; a worthless nag.

- A sorry woman. A word of contempt noting sometimes age, but generally vice.

- A young woman: in irony and slight contempt.

You see now and then some handsome young jades among them: the sluts have very often white teeth and black eyes. Add.

❧ The origin of *jade* is still unknown. It dates from 1386, when Chaucer referred to a horse in *The Canterbury Tales*. It became "a word of contempt" around 1560 but wasn't limited strictly to women; Shakespeare, for instance, used it for a man in *The Taming of the Shrew*. The word *jaded* comes from this sense of *jade* and originally meant "worn out like an old horse." ❧

jilt [*gilia*, Islandick, to intrap in an amour. Mr. Lye. Perhaps from *giglot*, by contraction; or *gillet*, or *gillot*, the diminutive of *gill*, the ludicrous name for a woman. 'Tis also called *jillet* in Scotland.]

- A woman who gives her lover hopes, and deceives him.

- A name of contempt for a woman.

❧ The etymology is a mystery: The *OED* editors speculate *jilt* might come from Jillet, the diminutive of the name Jill. The *OED* quotes Johnson's definition, "A woman who gives her lover hopes, and deceives him." ❧

jobbernówl [most probably from *jobbe*, Flemish, dull, and *nowl*, *knol*, Saxon, a head.] Loggerhead; blockhead.

❧ The word actually comes from the French *jobard*, "silly." ❧

jógger [from *jog*.] One who moves heavily and dully.

They, with their fellow joggers of the plough. Dryden.

jólthead [I know not whence derived.] A great head; a dolt; a blockhead.

Fie on thee, jolthead, thou can'st not read. Shakespeare.

❧ The origin of *jolthead* is still obscure. ❧

K

kite [*cyta*, Saxon.]

* A bird of prey that infests the farms, and steals the chickens.
* A name of reproach denoting rapacity.

Detested kite! thou liest. Shakes. King Lear.

knave [*cnapa*, Saxon.] A petty rascal; a soundrel; a dishonest fellow.

See all our fools aspiring to be knaves. Pope.

knuff [perhaps corrupted from *knave*, or the same with *chuff*.] A lout. An old word preserved in a rhyme of prediction.

The country knuffs, Hob, Dick, and Hick,
With clubs and clouted shoon,
Shall fill up Dussendale
With slaughtered bodies soon. Hayward.

❧ *Knuff* comes not from *knave* but from the Middle English *gnoff*, "a coarse, lumpish, or ill-mannered man." It first shows up in Chaucer's *Miller's Tale:* "A riche gnof, that gestes heeld to bord, / And of his craft he was a Carpenter." The "clouted shoon" in Sir John Hayward's poem are peasants' shoes held together with broad-headed nails, and the song celebrates the "Norfolk Rising" of 1549, when Robert Kett led a rebellion against greedy landowners. ⬥

L

laced mutton An old word for a whore.

❧ This slang term goes back at least to 1578. The *OED* defines *mutton* as "food for lust; loose women," and *laced* as probably meaning "wearing a bodice." Shakespeare used it in *Two Gentlemen of Verona*, but it was obsolete by the end of the seventeenth century. ⬥

láckbrain [*lack* and *brain*.] One that wants wit.

léwdster [from *lewd*.] A lecher; one given to criminal pleasures.

línseywoolsey [*linen* and *wool*.] Made of linen and wool mixed. Vile; mean; of different and unsuitable parts.

A lawless linseywoolsie brother,
Half of one order, half another. Hudibras, p. i.

Peel'd, patch'd and pyebald, linseywoolsey brothers,
Grave mummers! sleeveless some, and shirtless others. Pope's Dunciad,
   b. iii.

lob Any one heavy, clumsy, or sluggish.

Farewel, thou lob of spirits, I'll be gone,
Our queen and all her elves come here anon. Shakesp.

❦ Johnson puzzled over this word in editing Shakespeare's works. In
a footnote to *A Midsummer Night's Dream*, he explained Shakespeare's
phrase "lob of spirits": "*Lob, lubber, looby, lobcock,* all denote both in-
activity of body and dulness of mind." ❧

lóggerhead [*logge,* Dutch, stupid and *head,* or rather from *log,* a heavy
motionless mass, as blockhead.] A dolt; a blockhead; a thickscul.

lóiterer [from *loiter.*] A lingerer; an idler; a lazy wretch; one who lives
without business; one who is sluggish and dilatory.

Ever listless loit'rers, that attend
No cause, no trust, no duty, and no friend. Pope.

lóoby [Of this word the derivation is unsettled. Skinner mentions
lapp, German, *foolish;* and Junius, *llabe,* a clown, Welsh, which seems
to be the true original.] A lubber; a clumsy clown.

lósel [from *losian,* to perish.] A scoundrel; a sorry worthless fellow. A
word now obsolete.

lout [*loete*, old Dutch. Mr. Lye.] A mean aukward fellow; a bumpkin; a clown.

lown [*liun*, Irish; *loen*, Dutch, a stupid drone.] A scoundrel; a rascal.

> *King Stephen was a worthy peer,*
> *His breeches cost him but a crown,*
> *He thought them sixpence all too dear,*
> *And therefore call'd the taylor lown.* Shakespeare.

lowthóughted [*low* and *thought*.] Having the thoughts with-held from sublime or heavenly meditations; mean of sentiment; narrow mindedness.

lúbbard [from *lubber*.] A lazy sturdy fellow.

> *Yet their wine and their victuals those curmudgeon lubbards*
> *Lock up from my sight, in cellars and cupboards.* Swift.

lúbber [of this word the best derivation seems to be from *lubbed*, said by Junius to signify in Danish *fat*.] A sturdy drone; an idle, fat, bulky losel; a booby.

> *For tempest and showers deceiveth a many,*
> *And ling'ring lubbers loose many a penie.* Tusser's Husb.

⁌ *Lubber* comes from the Middle English *lobur*, "a lazy lout"; it may derive from the Old French *lobeor*, "a swindler." ⁍

lúmpish [from *lump*.] Heavy; gross; dull; unactive; bulky.

lusk [*lusche*, French.] Idle; lazy; worthless. Dict.

M

macaróon [*macarone*, Italian.] A coarse, rude, low fellow; whence *macaronick* poetry, in which the language is purposely corrupted.

❧ *Macaronic* poetry mixes languages, such as English and Latin. Johnson dismissed it as a "motley ludicrous species of composition." ❧

málapert [*mal* and *pert*.] Saucy; quick with impudence; sprightly without respect or decency.

If thou dar'st tempt me further, draw thy sword.
—*What, what? nay, then, I must have an ounce or two of this malapert blood from you.* Shakesp. Twelfth Night.

❧ Boswell could be short on "respect or decency" and occasionally got on Johnson's nerves. When pestered by a long barrage of impertinent questions—"What did you do, Sir?" "What did you say, Sir?"—Johnson "at last grew enraged" with Boswell's badgering and reprimanded him: "I will not be put to the *question*. Don't you consider, Sir, that these are not the manners of a gentleman? I will not be baited with *what*, and *why*; what is this? what is that? why is a cow's tail long? why is a fox's tail bushy?" Boswell, put out by this chiding, tried to appease him: "Why, Sir, you are so good, that I venture to trouble you." "Sir," snapped Johnson, "my being so *good* is no reason why you should be so *ill*." ❧

málkin [from *mal*, of *Mary*, and *kin*, the diminutive termination.] A kind of mop made of clouts for sweeping ovens; thence a frightful figure of clouts dressed up; thence a dirty wench. Hanmer.

> *The kitchen malkin pins*
> *Her richest lockram 'bout her reechy neck,*
> *Clamb'ring the walls to eye him.* Shakesp. Coriolanus.

málthorse [*malt* and *horse.*] It seems to have been, in Shakespeare's time, a term of reproach for a dull dolt.

You peasant swain, you whoreson, you malthorse drudge. Shakespeare's Taming of the Shrew.

malversátion [French.] Bad shifts; mean artifices; wicked and fraudulent tricks.

manháter [*man* and *hater.*] Misanthrope; one that hates mankind.

❧ Johnson didn't entertain high hopes for his species. "One can scarcely help wishing," he said, "while one fondles a baby, that it may never live to become a man; for it is *so* probable that when he becomes a man, he should be sure to end in a scoundrel." And when a lady asked whether man was naturally good, Johnson replied, "No, madam, no more than a wolf." Boswell wanted to make sure he understood him: "Nor no woman, sir?" "No, sir," came the reply. The lady was shocked: "This is worse than Swift." ☙

máwmish [from *mawm* or *mawmet.*] Foolish; idle; nauseous.

It is one of the most nauseous, mawmish mortifications, for a man of sense to have to do with a punctual, finical fop. L'Estrange.

méacock [*mes coq*, Skinner.] An uxorious or effeminate man.

❧ Skinner's guess on the origin of the word is wrong, but no one has a better suggestion. The *OED* suggests it might be a diminutive of the name Maud. ❧

merry-ándrew A buffoon; a zany; a jack-pudding.

He would be a statesman becáuse he is a buffoon; as if there went no more to the making of a counsellor than the faculties of a merry-andrew or tumbler. L'Estrange.

❧ When Boswell spoke up for actors—"You never will allow merit to a player"—Johnson cried, "Merit, Sir! what merit? . . . What, Sir, a fellow who claps a hump on his back, and a lump on his leg, and cries 'I am Richard the Third'?" Boswell wasn't convinced. "My dear Sir! you may turn anything into ridicule. . . . *Who* can repeat Hamlet's soliloquy, 'To be, or not to be,' as Garrick does it?" Johnson replied, "Any body may." Pointing at an eight-year-old boy in the room, he added, "Jemmy, there, will do it as well in a week." ❧

mílksop [*milk* and *sop*.] A soft, mild, effeminate, feeble-minded man.

A milksop, one that never in his life
Felt so much cold as over shoes in snow. Shak. Rich. III.

mínx [contracted, I suppose, from *minnock*.] A young, pert, wanton girl.

mome A dull, stupid blockhead, a stock, a post: this owes its original to the French word *momon*, which signifies the gaming at dice in masquerade, the custom and rule of which is, that a strict silence is to be observed; whatsoever sum one stakes another covers, but not a word is to be spoken; from hence also comes our word *mum* for silence. Hanmer.

Mome, malthorse, capon, coxcomb, idiot, patch!
Either get thee from the door, or sit down at the hatch. Shakespeare's
   Comedy of Errours.

moon-calf [*moon* and *calf.*]

* A monster; a false conception: supposed perhaps anciently to be produced by the influence of the moon.

* A dolt; a stupid fellow.

The potion works not on the part design'd,
But turns his brain, and stupifies his mind;
The sotted moon-calf gapes. Dryden's Juvenal.

to mop [from *mock.*] To make wry mouths in contempt.

Five fiends have been in poor Tom at once; of lust, as Obidicut; Hobbidi-
den, prince of dumbness; Mahu, of stealing; Mobu, of murder; and Flib-
bertigibbet, of mopping and mowing, who since possesses chamber-maids.
Shakesp.

mópus [A cant word from *mope.*] A drone; a dreamer.

móuth-friend [*mouth* and *friend.*] One who professes friendship with-out intending it.

❧ Boswell mentioned that a rich Scottish landlord always "left Skye with the blessings of his people," but Johnson reminded him that the professions of friendship weren't entirely heartfelt: "You'll observe this was when he *left* it. It is only the back of him that they bless."❧

múckworm [*muck* and *worm.*]

- A worm that lives in dung.

- A miser; a curmudgeon.

múshroom [*mouscheron*, French.] An upstart; a wretch risen from the dunghill; a director of a company.

❦It seems Shakespeare's contemporary Christopher Marlowe was the first to use *mushroom* as an insult in *Edward II:* "A night growne mushrump, Such a one as my Lord of Cornewall is." Why Johnson had it in for "a director of a company" is unclear.❧

N

nídget [corrupted from *nithing* or *niding.* The opprobrious term with which the man was anciently branded who refused to come to the royal standard in times of exigency.] A coward; a dastard.

There was one true English word of greater force than them all, now out of all use; it signifieth no more than abject, baseminded, false-hearted, coward, or nidget. Camden.

❦The word actually comes from *an idiot.* In the sixteenth century, speakers detached the n from *an* and moved it to the beginning of the next word, so *an idiot* became *a nidiot* and then *a nidget.*❧

níding [from *nið*, Saxon, vileness.] Niding, an old English word signifying abject, base-minded, false-hearted, coward, or nidget. Carew.

nímmer [from *nim*.] A thief; a pilferer.

nincompoop [A corruption of the Latin *non compos*.] A fool; a trifler.

An old ninnyhammer, a dotard, a nincompoop, is the best language she can afford me. Addison.

❧ Johnson's etymology is appealing but probably wrong. He suggests *nincompoop* comes from *non compos mentis*, Latin for "not sound in the mind, insane." But the earliest recorded uses of the word in the late seventeenth century spell it differently—*nicompoop* or *nickumpoop*—making the Latin derivation unlikely. It's a pity Johnson didn't live long enough to see Horace Walpole coin an eminently useful word in 1791, *nincompoophood.* ❧

nínny [*ninno*, a child, Spanish.] A fool; a simpleton.

❧ The *OED* guesses *ninny* came not from Spanish *niño* but from *an innocent.* ❧

nínnyhammer [from *ninny*.] A simpleton.

Have you no more manners than to rail at Hocus, that has saved that clod-pated, numskull'd, ninny-hammer of yours from ruin, and all his family. Arbuth. John Bull.

níthing A coward, dastard, poltroon.

nízy A dunce; a simpleton. A low word.

nóddle [*hnol,* Saxon.] A head; in contempt.

> *My head's not made of brass,*
> *As friar Bacon's noddle was.* Hudibras, p. ii. cant. 1.

nóddy [from *naudin,* French.] A simpleton; an idiot.

> *The whole race of bawling, fluttering noddies, by what title soever digni-*
> *fied, are akin to the ass in this fable.* L'Estrange, Fable 150.

noíer [from *noie.*] One who annoys. An old word in disuse.

> *The north is a noier to grass of all suits,*
> *The east a destroyer to herbs and all fruits.* Tuss. Husb.

❦Boswell, for all his charm, could be annoying, and sometimes Johnson found him too much to take. One night he asked too many questions, prompting Johnson to spit out, "Sir, you have but two topicks, yourself and me. I am sick of both."❧

noíous [*noioso,* Italian.] Hurtful; mischievous; troublesome; inconve‑nient. Obsolete.

> *But neither darkness foul, nor filthy bands,*
> *Nor noious smell his purpose could withhold.* Fairy Q.

nónsense [*non* and *sense.*] Trifles; things of no importance.

> *What's the world to him,*
> *'Tis nonsense all.* Thomson.

❦Boswell liked voicing oddball opinions just to see Johnson's reac‑tion. Sometimes Johnson took the bait, and sometimes he didn't. Once Boswell "attempted to argue for the superior happiness of the savage life," but Johnson wasn't in the mood. "No, Sir," he said, "you are not to talk such paradox: let me have no more on't." Johnson then referred to someone else who often praised the "savage life" as superior to modern civilization: "Lord Monboddo, one of your Scotch Judges, talked a great deal of such nonsense. I suffered *him*; but I will not suffer *you*." BOSWELL: "But, Sir, does not Rousseau talk such nonsense?" JOHNSON: "True, Sir; but Rousseau *knows* he is talking nonsense, and laughs at the world for staring at him. . . . A man who talks nonsense so well, must know that he is talking nonsense. But I am *afraid*, Monboddo does *not* know that he is talking nonsense."

nóodle [from *noddle* or *noddy.*] A fool; a simpleton.

A *noodle* was a fool before it became a kind of pasta. The *OED* gives the first example of this (unrelated) meaning of *noodle* from 1779, nearly a quarter century after Johnson completed his *Dictionary.*

númskull [Probably from *numb*, torpid, insensible, and *skull.*] A dullard; a dunce; a dolt; a blockhead.

Or toes and fingers, in this case,
Of Numskulls self should take the place. Prior.

O

oats [*aten*, Saxon.] A grain, which in England is generally given to horses, but in Scotland supports the people.

❦As soon as the *Dictionary* appeared, this became one of its most famous definitions, and it enraged Scots for decades. Johnson was unrepentant: "Why, I own, that by my definition of *oats* I meant to vex them."

And yet he was surrounded by Scots, not least Boswell himself—and his very first words to his future biographer were a put-down on Scotland. Boswell, insecure about his Scottish origins, was at Thomas Davies' bookshop in London on May 16, 1763, when the great author of the *Dictionary of the English Language* walked in. As Davies made the introduction, Boswell nervously whispered, "Don't tell him where I come from." Davies couldn't help himself: "From Scotland," he said mischievously. Boswell, flustered, tried to explain: "Mr. Johnson," he sputtered, "I do indeed come from Scotland, but I cannot help it." Johnson latched on to "come from," interpreting it not as "was born in" but as "got out of," and retorted, "That, Sir, I find, is what a very great many of your countrymen cannot help."

Sometimes he'd make fun of the Scottish countryside, baiting the Scots by insisting their country had no trees. To Hester Thrale he said, "Seeing Scotland, Madam, is only seeing a worse England." When a Scottish friend insisted "Scotland had a great many noble wild prospects," Johnson agreed that there were beautiful prospects aplenty; "But, Sir, let me tell you, the noblest prospect which a Scotchman ever sees, is the high road that leads him to England!" Someone insisted that God made Scotland. "Certainly he did," said Johnson; "but we must always remember that he made it for Scotchmen." Besides, he added wickedly, "God made hell."

Even more fun than ridiculing Scotland was ridiculing the Scots. "The impudence of an Irishman is the impudence of a fly, that buzzes about you, and you put it away, but it returns again, and flutters and teazes you. The impudence of a Scotsman is the impudence of a leech, that fixes and sucks your blood." He gave his closest Scottish friend this backhanded compliment: "I will do you, Boswell, the justice to say, that you are the most *unscottified* of your countrymen. You are almost the only instance of a Scotchman that I have known, who did not at every other sentence bring in some other Scotchman."

Someone once asked him why he hated the Scots so much. "You are mistaken, Sir," he said; "I do not hate the Scotch; neither do I hate frogs, provided they keep in their *native element*; but I do not like to have them hopping about my bedchamber."

Why *did* he make fun of the Scots? Boswell once asked him directly: "Pray, Sir, can you trace the cause of your antipathy to the Scotch?" Johnson's answer was simple: "I can not, Sir." And most of his jeers were all in fun. Even the great Englishman sometimes ate Scottish oatmeal; he admitted to Boswell "that he too was fond of it when a boy." Boswell rejoiced.

óysterwench, óysterwoman [*oyster* and *wench*, or *woman*.] A woman whose business is to sell oysters. Proverbially. A low woman.

Off goes his bonnet to an oysterwench. Shakesp.

Oysterwomen show up in many eighteenth-century works as "low women." One of Thomas D'Urfey's naughty ballads from 1719, "While

óysterwench

Oyster Nan Stood by Her Tub," describes a dirty and dirty-minded woman—a "Flat-capt Fusby," he calls her—who ducks behind the barn with a vintner and nine months later finds herself the target of lewd jokes. ❧

P

pánder [This word is derived from *Pandarus*, the pimp in the story of Troilus and Cressida; it was therefore originally written *pandar*, till its etymology was forgotten.] A pimp; a male bawd; a procurer.

If thou fear to strike, and to make me certain it is done, thou art the pander to her dishonour, and equally to me disloyal. Shakesp. Cymbeline.

patch [*pezzo*, Italian.] A paltry fellow. Obsolete.

What a py'd ninny's this? thou scurvy patch! Shakesp.

pátriot One whose ruling passion is the love of his country.

❧ "Patriotism," said Johnson in one of his most memorable quotations, "is the last refuge of a scoundrel." Many think the line appears in the *Dictionary*: Ambrose Bierce's *Devil's Dictionary* mistakenly reports, "In Dr. Johnson's famous dictionary patriotism is defined as the last resort of a scoundrel." ("With all due respect to an enlightened but inferior lexicographer," Bierce adds, "I beg to submit that it is the first.") But the *Dictionary* definition of *patriot* is tame, and the famous jab at jingoism appears in Boswell's *Life*. Boswell was eager to clarify his meaning: "He did not mean a real and generous love of our country, but that pretended patriotism which so many, in all ages and countries, have made a cloak for self-interest." ▓

pátron [*patron*, Fr. *patronus*, Latin.] One who countenances, supports or protects. Commonly a wretch who supports with insolence, and is paid with flattery.

▓ The animosity behind this definition makes sense in the context of Johnson's work on the *Dictionary*. Johnson approached Philip Dormer Stanhope, the fourth earl of Chesterfield, in the hopes of securing his patronage—that is, financial backing; in return, Johnson would dedicate the book to him. But Chesterfield, unimpressed by the inelegant scholar, brushed him off with just ten pounds, and Johnson was forced to go it alone. Shortly before the *Dictionary* appeared, the word on the street was that Johnson's book was going to be a monument of scholarship. Chesterfield decided he wanted in on it, and started praising Johnson in the newspapers, hoping to get the dedication he hadn't earned.

Johnson was too proud for that, especially after completing the *Dictionary* "without one Act of assistance, one word of encouragement, or one smile of favour." He wrote a long note, one of the nastiest letters ever written by anyone, which includes this charge: "Is not a Patron, my Lord, one who looks with unconcern on a man struggling for life in the water, and, when he has reached ground, encumbers him with help?" And he remembered Chesterfield's slights for a long time. "This man," he said later, "I thought had been a Lord among wits; but, I find, he is only a wit among Lords!" He added that

Chesterfield's famous *Letters to His Son*, explaining to the young man how to behave in high society, "teach the morals of a whore, and the manners of a dancing master." ❧

pélting This word in Shakespeare signifies, I know not why, mean; paltry; pitiful.

> *Could great men thunder, Jove could ne'er be quiet;*
> *For every pelting petty officer*
> *Would use his heav'n for thunder.* Shakespeare.

❦ The origin of *pelting* remains unknown. ❧

pénsion [*pension*, Fr.] An allowance made to any one without an equivalent. In England it is generally understood to mean pay given to a state hireling for treason to his country.

> *He has liv'd with the great without flattery, and been a friend to men in power without pensions.* Pope.

❦ After a definition like this, dismissing those who receive government money as immoral hacks, it came as an embarrassment when Johnson himself received a pension in 1762. His critics, including the satirical poet Charles Churchill, were ecstatic at the opportunity to accuse him of hypocrisy. But Johnson dismissed the complaints as "a mighty foolish noise that they make." In fact, he loved a brawl so much that he told Boswell, "I wish my pension were twice as large, that they might make twice as much noise." ❧

pervicácious [*pervicax*, Lat.] Spitefully obstinate; peevishly contumacious.

pettifógger [corrupted from *pettivoguer; petit* and *voguer,* Fr.] A petty small-rate lawyer.

Physicians are apt to despise empiricks, lawyers, pettifoggers, merchants and pedlars. Swift.

Who can resist a good lawyer joke? Many of Johnson's best friends were lawyers (including Boswell), and Johnson considered the profession for himself. But on being asked about someone who left the room, he said that "he did not care to speak ill of any man behind his back, but"—he added conspiratorially—"he believed the gentleman was an *attorney.*"

píckleherring [*pickle* and *herring.*] A jack-pudding; a merry-andrew; a zany; a buffoon.

pickthánk [*pick* and *thank.*] An officious fellow, who does what he is not desired; a whispering parasite.

The business of a pickthank is the basest of offices. L'Estrange.

pláguy [from *plague.*] Vexatious; troublesome. A low word.

Plaguy was one of the favorite filler words of the eighteenth-century man-about-town, operating much like *damn* in the United States or *bloody* in England today. Anything that needed disparagement or emphasis could be called *plaguy.* Hester Thrale filled her diaries with phrases like "A foreign Nobleman is so plaguy touchy" and "She is plaguy nice that I can tell you." It's hard to find a comic play or novel of the era that doesn't use this "low word": John Gay's *Beggar's Opera* tells us women of spirit make "charming Mistresses, but plaguy Wives"; Oliver Goldsmith warned, "Don't be in such a plaguy hurry!"; Richard Brinsley Sheridan has a character who "looks plaguy gruff"; and Frances Burney's *Evelina* insists, "Half of [your faces] are plaguy ugly,—and, as to t'other half,—I believe it's none of God's manufactory."❧

poetáster [Latin.] A vile petty poet.

Horace hath exposed those trifling poetasters, that spend themselves in glaring descriptions, and sewing here and there some cloth of gold on their sackcloth. Felton.

❦ Eighteenth-century London was swarming with "vile petty poets," and Johnson crossed swords with many of them. Sometimes he ridiculed the satirical poet Charles Churchill, but Boswell thought that "he was not quite a fair judge" because Churchill had made fun of Johnson. "Nay, Sir," Johnson objected, "I am a very fair judge. He did not attack me violently till he found I did not like his poetry. . . . I called the fellow a blockhead at first, and I will call him a blockhead still." As for Edward Young, a superstar poet of the day, his poems "are but like bright steppingstones over a miry road: Young froths, and foams, and bubbles sometimes very vigorously; but we must not compare the noise made by your tea-kettle here with the roaring of the ocean." And Johnson may hold the record for the shortest book review ever. James Grainger read aloud from *The Sugar Cane*, his long georgic poem on the techniques of harvesting. When he came to a famous line—"Say, shall I sing of Rats?"—Johnson interrupted him: "No!"❧

politicáster A petty ignorant pretender to politicks.

There are quacks of all sorts; as bullies, pedants, hypocrites, empiricks, law jobbers and politicasters. L'Estrange.

❧For all his reputation as a belligerent Tory, Johnson had little patience for political discussions and dismissed political theories as bunk. Boswell thought it curious: "So, Sir, you laugh at schemes of political improvement." "Why, Sir," answered Johnson, "most schemes of political improvement are very laughable things." Late in life, when Johnson's health was bad, Boswell tried to strike up a political conversation. "Sir," Johnson replied, "I'd as soon have a man to break my bones as talk to me of publick affairs, internal or external. I have lived to see things all as bad as they can be." But this cynicism wasn't entirely a result of old age—years earlier he had produced an admirably direct summary of the politicians of his, or perhaps any, age: "The characteristick of our own government at present is imbecility."❧

póltron [*pollice truncato*, from the thumb cut off; it being once a practice of cowards to cut off their thumbs, that they might not be compelled to serve in war. Saumaise. Menage derives it from the Italian *poltro*, a bed; as cowards feign themselves sick a bed: others derive it from *polctro* or *poltro*, a young unbroken horse.] A coward; a nidgit; a scoundrel.

Patience is for poltrons. Shakesp.

❧The etymology proposed by the seventeenth-century scholar Claude Saumaise, with cowards cutting off their own thumbs, is a wonderful story, but there's nothing to it. *Poltron* (or *poltroon*) comes from the French *poltron* or Italian *poltrone*, and it's probably derived from *poltro*, "a young unbroken horse."❧

pox [properly *pocks*, which originally signified a small bag or pustule; of the same original, perhaps, with *powke* or *pouch*. We still use *pock*, for a single pustule; *poccas*, Sax. *pocken*, Dutch.]

- Pustules; efflorescencies; exanthematous eruptions.
- The venereal disease. This is the sense when it has no epithet.

❦ Johnson has no note on it, but *pox* was an oath that could make anything sound worse. Shakespeare was fond of it: "A pox of that jest!" says Katharine in *Love's Labour's Lost*, and in *All's Well That Ends Well* Bertram spits out, "A pox on him, he's a cat still." It became even more fashionable in the eighteenth century. In Pope's mock-epic *Rape of the Lock*, the notoriously inarticulate Sir Plume offers these words of wisdom: "My Lord, why, what the Devil? / Zounds! damn the Lock! 'fore Gad, you must be civil! / Plague on't! 'tis past a Jest—nay prithee, Pox!" ❦

prig [A cant word derived perhaps from *prick*, as he *pricks* up, he is *pert*; or from *prickeared*, an epithet of reproach bestowed upon the presbyterian teachers.] A pert, conceited, saucy, pragmatical, little fellow.

There have I seen some active prig,
To shew his parts, bestride a twig. Swift's Miscel.

❦ The "presbyterian teachers" were the Puritans, known in the seventeenth century for close-cropped hair that made their ears visible. It's unclear whether that's the real origin of *prig*. The writer William Mason once brought a frivolous lawsuit against the bookseller John Murray over a matter of copyright, and Johnson attacked him: "Mason's a Whig." His friend Mrs. Knowles was nearby but couldn't hear him clearly: "What! a Prig, Sir?" Johnson burst out laughing: "Worse, Madam; a Whig!" He then added, "But he is both." ❦

punch [*Punctilio obesus*, Lat.] In contempt or ridicule, a short fat fellow.

⟨Johnson's etymology is probably wrong; it seems to come from Punchinello, the puppet-show character, whose name was shortened to Punch. The *OED* says *punch* came to be "applied to any person, animal, or thing, thought to resemble the puppet, esp. in being short and stout." Punchinello later gave his name to *Punch*, the British humor magazine that ran from 1841 until 1992.⟩

púndle [*mulier pumila & obesa*, Lat.] A short and fat woman. Ainsworth.

punk A whore; a common prostitute; a strumpet.

She may be a punk; for many of them are neither maid, widow, nor wife. Shakesp. Measure for Measure.

And made them fight, like mad or drunk,
For dame religion as for punk. Hudibras.

púnster [from *pun*.] A quibbler; a low wit who endeavours at reputation by double meaning.

⟨Johnson, like many of his contemporaries, dismissed puns as "false wit" and rarely had anything kind to say about wordplay. But he made a few exceptions. When Hester Thrale praised a friend, the coxcomical Dudley Long, Johnson shot back, "Nay, my dear lady, don't talk so. Mr. Long's character is very *short*. It is nothing." Fishing about for something good to say about him, he came up with no more than "He fills a chair."⟩

púppet [*poupée*, Fr. *pupus*, Lat.]

- A small image moved by men in a mock drama; a wooden tragedian.
- A word of contempt.

Thou, an Egyptian puppet, shalt be shewn
In Rome as well as I. Shakesp. Cymbeline.

púppy [*poupée*, Fr.]

* A whelp; progeny of a bitch.

* A name of contemptuous reproach to a man.

I shall laugh myself to death at this puppy headed monster; a most scurvy
monster! Shakesp. Tempest.

❧ Once while browsing a new translation of the New Testament, Johnson opened to John 11:35: "Jesus wept." But the translator, eager to show off his literary skills, rendered this passage, "And Jesus, the Saviour of the world, burst into a flood of tears." Johnson "contemptuously threw the book aside, exclaiming, 'Puppy!'"

As a boy, he found himself on the receiving end of this insult. He always had trouble with authority figures, and his sharp tongue often got him into trouble. When the young Sam misbehaved, his mother called him a puppy. The son's reply? "I asked her if she knew what they called a puppy's mother." ❧

púrsy [*poussif*, Fr.] Shortbreathed and fat.

   By these, the Medes
Perfume their breaths, and cure old pursy men. Temple.

pútid [*putidus*, Lat.] Mean; low; worthless.

Q

quean [*cwean*, Saxon, a barren cow; *Horcwen*, in the laws of Canute, a strumpet.] A worthless woman, generally a strumpet.

This well they understand like cunning queans,
And hide their nastiness behind the scenes. Dryden.

R

ragamúffin [from *rag* and I know not what else.] A paltry mean fellow.

Shall we brook that paltry ass
And feeble scoundrel, Hudibras,
With that more paltry ragamuffin,
Ralpho, vapouring and huffing. Hudibras, p. i.

❦ The *American Heritage Dictionary* traces *ragamuffin* to Ragamoffyn, a demon in William Langland's fourteenth-century poem *Piers Plowman*; whether *ragamuffin* comes from Ragamoffyn or the other way around isn't clear. The *OED* suggests the word is from *rag* with a "fanciful ending." ❦

rake [*Racaille*, Fr. the low rabble; or *rekel*, Dutch, a worthless cur dog.] A loose, disorderly, vicious, wild, gay, thoughtless fellow; a man addicted to pleasure.

Men, some to bus'ness, some to pleasure take;
But ev'ry woman is at heart a rake. Pope.

rákehel [of this word the etymology is doubtful: as it is now written, it is apparently derived from *rake* and *hell*, and may aptly represent a wretch whose life is passed in places of lewdness and wickedness: Skinner derives it from *racaille*, French, the rabble; Junius, from *rekel*, Dutch, a mongrel dog.] A wild, worthless, dissolute, debauched, sorry fellow.

rampállian A mean wretch. Not in use.

Away you scullion, you rampallian, you fustilarian. Shak.

rántipole [this word is wantonly formed from *rant*.] Wild; roving; rakish. A low word.

ráscal [*rascal*, Saxon, a lean beast.] A mean fellow; a scoundrel; a sorry wretch.

I am accurst to rob in that thief's company; the rascal hath remov'd my horse. Shakesp. Henry IV. p. i.

❧ Johnson went after rascals of every stripe, and he'd use the word for even minor offenses, as when a waiter "put a lump of sugar with his fingers into Dr. Johnson's lemonade." But he took particular pleasure in attacking one group of rascals: Americans. On this subject Johnson was always "a violent aggressor," saying, "I am willing to love all mankind, *except an American.*" Boswell writes that "his inflammable corruption bursting into horrid fire, he 'breathed out threatenings and slaughter'; calling them, 'Rascals—Robbers—Pirates'; and exclaiming, he'd 'burn and destroy them.'" "Sir," he said, "they are a race of convicts, and ought to be thankful for anything we allow them short of hanging."

His complaints with America came from many sources, but foremost among them was the practice of slavery—Johnson was one of the leading abolitionists of his age. On this topic his language was always forceful, as when he called Jamaica "a place of great wealth and dreadful wickedness, a den of tyrants and a dungeon of slaves." On learning of the death of a Jamaican planter and slaveholder, Johnson said, "He will not, whither he is now gone, find much difference, I believe, either in the climate or the company."❧

rascálity [from *rascal*.] The low mean people.

rédcoat A name of contempt for a soldier.

The fearful passenger, who travels late,
Shakes at the moon-shine shadow of a rush,
And sees a redcoat rise from ev'ry bush. Dryden.

❧ The use of *redcoat* for a soldier goes back to 1520, but it became "a name of contempt" only in Johnson's lifetime. The American colonists latched on to it to single out the hated British soldiers—even though, on the topic of America, Johnson sided firmly with the redcoats.❧

réprobate A man lost to virtue; a wretch abandoned to wickedness.

I acknowledge myself for a reprobate, a villain, a traytor to the king, and the most unworthy man that ever lived. Ral.

repúblican [from *republick*.] One who thinks a commonwealth without monarchy the best government.

*These people are more happy in imagination than the rest of their
neighbours, because they think themselves so; though such a chimerical
happiness is not peculiar to republicans.* Add.

❧ Johnson was a firm supporter of the monarchy, and even when he
disliked the king on the throne, he stood up for the institution. He
therefore had harsh words for people like the historian Catherine
Macaulay, who believed in tearing down social hierarchies. Johnson
visited her one day and decided to bluff: "Madam," he said, "I am now
become a convert to your way of thinking. I am convinced that all
mankind are upon an equal footing." He then invited her servants to
sit down to dinner with her—and watched her egalitarian principles
evaporate in a fit of snobbery. Johnson told Boswell, "I thus, Sir,
shewed her the absurdity of the levelling doctrine. She has never liked
me since. Sir, your levellers wish to level *down* as far as themselves; but
they cannot bear levelling *up* to themselves. They would all have some
people under them; why not then have some people above them?"

But the most notorious republican was the poet John Milton,
who joined with the rebels who executed Charles I in 1649. Though
Johnson praised *Paradise Lost*, he had no truck with Milton's politics.
His "political notions," he wrote in his *Life* of the poet, "were those
of an acrimonious and surly republican. . . . Milton's republicanism
was, I am afraid, founded in an envious hatred of greatness, and a
sullen desire of independence; in petulance impatient of controul,
and pride disdainful of superiority. He hated monarchs in the state
and prelates in the church; for he hated all whom he was required to
obey. It is to be suspected that his predominant desire was to destroy
rather than establish, and that he felt not so much the love of liberty
as repugnance to authority."

Milton's works therefore come in for serious abuse. His famous pastoral elegy *Lycidas* was "easy, vulgar, and therefore disgusting." Even a work as great as *Paradise Lost* wasn't beyond criticism. Johnson called it the second-greatest epic ever written, but still said it's "one of the books which the reader admires and lays down, and forgets to take up again. None ever wished it longer than it is." (He thought only three books should be longer than they were: *Don Quixote, Robinson Crusoe,* and *The Pilgrim's Progress.*) ❧

rhýmer, rhýmster [from *rhyme.*] One who makes rhymes; a versifier; a poet in contempt.

His rhime is constrained at an age, when the passion of love makes every man a rhimer, though not a poet. Dryden.

❧ Johnson often talked about poets in contempt. He had this cutting review of a new translation of the Roman poet Martial: "There are in these verses too much folly for madness, I think, and too much madness for folly." In a debate over whether Samuel Derrick or Christopher Smart was the better poet, Johnson offered the following verdict, flattering to neither: "Sir, there is no settling the point of precedency between a louse and a flea." ❧

rodomontáde [from a boastful boisterous hero of Ariosto, called *Rodomonte; rodomontade,* Fr.] An empty noisy bluster or boast; a rant.

roíster, or **roísterer** [from the verb.] A turbulent, brutal, lawless, blustering fellow.

rónion [I know not the etymology, nor certainly the meaning of this word.] A fat bulky woman.

❧The *OED* is no help on this one: "Of uncertain origin." Johnson had to guess the meaning from context.❧

róynish [*rogneux*, Fr. mangy, paltry.] Paltry; sorry; mean; rude.

rúffian [*ruffiano*, Italian; *ruffien*, Fr. a bawd; *roffver*, Danish, to pillage; perhaps it may be best derived from *rough*.] A brutal, boisterous, mischievous fellow; a cutthroat; a robber; a murderer.

❧Johnson singled out one "ruffian" above all others: James Macpherson. This Scottish poet published translations of long-lost epic poems by the ancient bard Ossian, and for a while critics were thrilled, declaring them better than those by Homer and Virgil. But Johnson wasn't impressed. Not only did he say they were bad; he insisted they were phony, and that Ossian never existed.

Macpherson had his defenders; one, the critic Hugh Blair, asked Johnson "whether he thought any man of a modern age could have written such poems." "Yes, Sir," Johnson said; "many men, many women, and many children." It was easy to turn out such poetic nonsense all day long without effort: "Sir," he said, "a man might write such stuff for ever, if he would *abandon* his mind to it."

The battle over Ossian prompted one of Johnson's nastiest letters, second only to his assault on Lord Chesterfield (see **patron**). When Johnson declared the epics were fakes, the hotheaded Macpherson responded with threats of physical harm. Johnson took to carrying "an oak-plant of tremendous size" to ward off Macpherson's goons, and he sent back this belligerent reply: "I received your foolish and impudent letter. Any violence offered me I shall do my best to repel; and what I cannot do for myself, the law shall do for me. I hope I shall never be deterred from detecting what I think a cheat, by the menaces of a ruffian. . . . I thought your book an imposture; I think it an imposture still. . . . Your rage I defy. Your abilities . . . are not so formidable; and what I hear of your morals inclines me to pay regard not to what you shall say, but to what you shall prove. You may print this if you will."⟩

rúnnion [*rognant*, Fr. scrubbing.] A paltry scurvy wretch.

You witch! you poulcat! you runnion! Shakesp.

S

sábbathbreaker [*sabbath* and *break*.] Violator of the sabbath by labour or wickedness.

⟨Religion was a serious matter for the devout Johnson, and the movement known as the Enlightenment—in French, *lumières*—was too atheistic to please him. When he attacked one of these "freethinkers," someone replied, "Allow him the *lumières* at least." "I do allow him, Sir, just enough to light him to hell." Sometimes his jabs could be elegantly to the point. When someone tried to introduce Johnson to Guillaume-Thomas Raynal, notorious for his infidelity—"Will you permit me, Sir, to present to you the Abbé Reynal?"—Johnson's reply was simply a loud "*No, Sir.*"⟩

sáucebox [from *sauce*, or rather from *saucy*.] An impertinent or petulant fellow.

scámbler [Scottish.] A bold intruder upon one's generosity or table.

scélerat [French; *sceleratus*, Latin.] A villain; a wicked wretch. A word introduced unnecessarily from the French by a Scottish author.

    ❦ The Scottish author seems to be George Cheyne, a medical writer. Johnson advised Boswell to read his book *The English Malady* but added, "I would not have you read any thing else of Cheyne." ❦

scíolous [*sciolus*, Latin.] Superficially or imperfectly knowing.

    I could wish these sciolous zelotists had more judgment joined with their zeal. Howel.

scold [from the verb.] A clamourous, rude, mean, low, foul-mouthed woman.

    A shrew in domestick life, is now become a scold in politicks. Addison's Freeholder.

scomm [Perhaps from *scomma*, Latin.] A buffoon. A word out of use, and unworthy of revival.

to sconce [A word used in the universities, and derived plausibly by Skinner, whose etymologies are generally rational, from *sconce*, as it signifies the head; to *sconce* being to fix a fine on any one's head.] To mulct; to fine. A low word which ought not to be retained.

    ❦ It's odd to think of the great scholar as an unruly student. But Johnson spent much of his all-too-brief time at Oxford skipping lectures, when the custom was to fine (or "mulct") students two pence for each missed class. Johnson, once caught by his tutor and made to pay the fine, delivered this deliciously insolent comeback: "Sir, you have sconced me two-pence for nonattendance at a lecture not worth a penny."

scóundrel [*scondaruolo*, Italian, a hider. Skinner.] A mean rascal; a low petty villain.

Boswell observed that Johnson "used the epithet *scoundrel* very commonly, not quite in the sense in which it is generally understood, but as a strong term of disapprobation." Just about anyone who irritated him was a scoundrel: politicians were scoundrels, rabble-rousers were scoundrels, cowards were scoundrels, sick people were scoundrels, and "whoever thinks of going to bed before twelve o'clock is a scoundrel."

scráper [from *scrape*.]

+ A miser; a man intent on getting money; a scrapepenny.

+ A vile fiddler.

A fiddler didn't have to be "vile" to earn Johnson's scorn. While he sat bored through a concert, a friend whispered to him that the famous violinist was performing a very difficult piece. "Difficult do you call it, Sir?—I wish it were impossible."

scríbbler [from *scribble*.] A petty author; a writer without worth.

The most copious writers are the arrantest scribblers, and in so much talking the tongue runs before the wit. L'Estrange.

When a friend said of a new play, "We have hardly a right to abuse this tragedy; for bad as it is, how vain should either of us be to write one not near so good," Johnson corrected him: "Why no, Sir; this is not just reasoning. You *may* abuse a tragedy, though you cannot write one. You may scold a carpenter who has made you a bad table, though you cannot make a table. It is not your trade to make tables."

And abuse he did, often with astonishing bluntness. He said of one book, "If you should search all the mad-houses in England, you would not find ten men who would write so, and think it sense." Even friends weren't immune. He knew Elizabeth Montagu, called "the Queen of the Blues" for being the center of the Bluestocking Circle of learned women. But he wasn't impressed by her *Essay on Shakespeare*. Sir Joshua Reynolds spoke up for it: "I think that essay does her honour." "Yes, Sir," said Johnson; "it does *her* honour, but it would do nobody else honour."

Nor did Lord Lyttelton's *Dialogues of the Dead* do a useful service: "That man sat down to write a book, to tell the world what the world had all his life been telling him." And Johnson refused to meet the author Hugh Kelly, explaining, "I never desire to converse with a man who has written more than he has read."

He especially enjoyed making heretical comments on famous writers. Henry Fielding, the author of *Tom Jones* and one of England's greatest novelists, was "a blockhead." Jonathan Swift's masterpiece, *Gulliver's Travels*, didn't impress him: "When once you have thought of big men and little men, it is very easy to do all the rest." And though he adored Shakespeare, he could raise hackles by criticizing even the Bard: "Shakespeare never has six lines together without a fault." ❧

scroyle [This word I remember only in Shakespeare: it seems derived from *escrouelle*, French, a scrofulous swelling; as he calls a mean fellow a *scab* from his itch, or a *patch* from his raggedness.] A mean fellow; a rascal; a wretch.

> *The scroyles of Angiers flout you kings,*
> *And stand securely on their battlements,*
> *As in a theatre.* Shakespeare's King John.

❧ The *OED* rejects Johnson's suggestion of *escrouelle* but has nothing better to offer in its place. It's not only Shakespeare's word; it appears also in the works of Ben Jonson and the poet John Taylor. ❧

scrúbbed, scrúbby [*scrubet*, Danish.] Mean; vile; worthless; dirty; sorry.

> *I gave it to a youth,*
> *A kind of boy, a little scrubbed boy,*
> *No higher than thyself.* Shak. Merchant of Venice.

> *The scrubbiest cur in all the pack,*
> *Can set the mastiff on your back.* Swift.

scúlker [from *sculk*.] A lurker; one that hides himself for shame or mischief.

scúllion [from *escueille*, French, a dish.] The lowest domestick servant, that washes the kettles and the dishes in the kitchen.

> *I must, like a whore, unpack*
> *my heart with words,*

scúllion

And fall a cursing like a very drab,
A scullion, fye upon 't! foh! about my brain. Shak. Hamlet.

scúrril [*scurrilis*, Latin.] Low; mean; grosly opprobrious; loudly jocose.

> *With him, Patroclus,*
> *Upon a lazy bed, the live-long day*
> *Breaks scurril jests.* Shakesp. Troilus and Cressida.

séeksorrow [*seek* and *sorrow*.] One who contrives to give himself vexation.

shábby [A word that has crept into conversation and low writing; but ought not to be admitted into the language.] Mean; paltry.

> *The dean was so shabby, and look'd like a ninny,*
> *That the captain suppos'd he was curate to Jenny.* Swift.

shállowbrained [*shallow* and *brain*.] Foolish; futile; trifling; empty.

> *It cannot but be matter of just indignation to all good men to see a company of lewd shallowbrained huffs making atheism, and contempt of religion, the sole badge of wit.* South.

shámmer [from *sham*.] A cheat; an impostor. A low word.

shárper [from *sharp*.] A tricking fellow; a petty thief; a rascal.

sháveling [from *shave*.] A man shaved; a friar, or religious. Used in contempt.

> *Of elfes, there be no such things; only by bald fryars and knavish shavelings so feigned.* Spenser.

shéepbiter [from *sheepbite.*] A petty thief.

> *There are political sheepbiters as well as pastoral: betrayers of publick trusts, as well as of private.* L'Estrange.

símpless [*simplesse*, French.] Simplicity; silliness; folly. An obsolete word.

sin [*syn*, Saxon.] It is used by Shakespeare emphatically for a man enormously wicked.

> *Thy ambition,*
> *Thou scarlet sin, robb'd this bewailing land*
> *Of noble Buckingham.* Shakespeare's Henry VIII.

sínworm [*sin* and *worm.*] A vile sinful creature.

sírrah [*sir, ha!* Minshew.] A compellation of reproach and insult.

> *Sirrah, there's no room for faith, troth, or honesty in this bosom of thine.* Shakespeare's Henry IV.

skípjack [*skip* and *jack.*] An upstart.

> *The want of shame or brains does not presently entitle every little skipjack to the board's-end in the cabinet.* L'Estr.

sláverer [*slabbaerd*, Dutch; from *slaver.*] One who cannot hold his spittle; a driveller; an ideot.

slúbberdegullion [I suppose a cant word without derivation.] A paltry, dirty, sorry wretch.

slug [*slug*, Danish, and *slock*, Dutch, signify a glutton, and thence one that has the sloth of a glutton.] An idler; a drone; a slow, heavy, sleepy, lazy wretch.

to slúggardize [from *sluggard*.] To make idle; to make dronish.

> *Rather see the wonders of the world abroad,*
> *Than, living dully sluggardiz'd at home,*
> *Wear out thy youth with shapeless idleness.* Shakespeare.

sméllfeast [*smell* and *feast*.] A parasite; one who haunts good tables.

> *The ant lives upon her own, honestly gotten; whereas the fly is an*
> *intruder, and a common smellfeast that spunges upon other people's*
> *trenchers.* L'Estrange.

snéakup [from *sneak*.] A cowardly, creeping, insidious scoundrel. Obsolete.

> *The prince is a jack, a sneakup; and, if he were here, I would cudgel him*
> *like a dog, if he would say so.* Shak. H. IV.

sníveller [from *snivel*.] A weeper; a weak lamenter.

> *He'd more lament when I was dead,*
> *Than all the snivellers round my bed.* Swift.

sóphister [*sophiste*, French; *sophista*, Latin.] A disputant fallaciously subtle; an artful but insidious logician.

> *A subtle traitor needs no sophister.* Shakespeare's Hen. VI.

sot [*sot*, Saxon; *sot*, French; *sot*, Dutch.]

- A blockhead; a dull ignorant stupid fellow; a dolt.
- A wretch stupified by drinking.

soúlless [from *soul*.] Mean; low; spiritless.

Slave, soulless villain, dog, O rarely base! Shakespeare.

spániel [*hispaniolus*, Latin; *espagneul*, French.]

- A dog used for sports in the field, remarkable for sagacity and obedience.
- A low, mean, sneaking fellow; a courtier; a dedicator; a pensioner; a dependant; a placeman.

   I mean sweet words,
Low crooked curtesies, and base spaniel fawning. Shakesp.

   I am your spaniel; and, Demetrius,
The more you beat me I will fawn on you. Shakespeare.

spark [*spearca*, Saxon; *sparke*, Dutch.] A lively, showy, splendid, gay man. It is commonly used in contempt.

Unlucky as Fungoso in the play,
These sparks with aukward vanity display
What the fine gentlemen wore yesterday. Pope.

spónger [from *sponge*.] One who hangs for a maintenance on others.

A generous rich man, that kept a splendid and open table, would try which were friends, and which only trencher-flies and spungers. L'Estrange.

státeswoman [*state* and *woman.*] A woman who meddles with publick affairs. In contempt.

Several objects may innocently be ridiculed, as the passions of our stateswomen. Addison.

❖ When Boswell accused Johnson of making "a certain political lady" look ridiculous—he meant Catherine Macaulay, a historian famous for her republican political views—Johnson laughed. "That was already done, Sir. To endeavour to make *her* ridiculous, is like blacking the chimney." On another occasion, on hearing that Macaulay "had of late become very fond of dress, sat hours together at her toilet [dressing table], and even put on rouge," Johnson replied, "She is better employed at her toilet, than using her pen. It is better she should be reddening her own cheeks, than blackening other people's characters." ❖

stínkard [from *stink.*] A mean stinking paltry fellow.

stóckjobber [*stock* and *job.*] A low wretch who gets money by buying and selling shares in the funds.

The stockjobber thus from 'Change-alley goes down,
And tips you the freeman a wink;
Let me have but your vote to serve for the town,
And here is a guinea to drink. Swift.

❖ Johnson was more or less a capitalist and a friend of the first theorist of modern-day capitalism, Adam Smith. But moneygrubbing disgusted him. Perhaps it had something to do with his dislike of the Whigs, the party of commercial expansion. Old Whigs, he admitted, were principled, but modern-day Whiggism "was no better than the politicks of stock-jobbers, and the religion of infidels." ❖

strápping Vast; large; bulky. Used of large men or women in contempt.

stuff [*stoffe*, Dutch; *estoffe*, French.] Matter or thing. It is now seldom used in any sense but in contempt or dislike.

> *Such stuff as madmen*
> *Tongue and brain not.* Shakespeare.

> *Please not thyself the flatt'ring crowd to hear,*
> *'Tis fulsome stuff to feed thy itching ear.* Dryden's Pers.

> *To-morrow will be time enough*
> *To hear such mortifying stuff.* Swift.

stultíloquence [*stultus* and *loquentia*, Lat.] Foolish talk. Dict.

T

tarpáwling [from *tar*.] A sailor in contempt.

> *Was any thing wanting to the extravagance of this age, but the making a living tarpawlin and a swabber the hero of a tragedy.* Dennis.

❦ Johnson was no fan of the ocean. On his tour of the Scottish islands with Boswell in 1773, his boat almost went down in a storm. On his one trip outside Britain, a journey to France with the Thrales in 1775, he suffered from seasickness even on calm seas. Perhaps experiences like that prompted him to say, "No man will be a sailor, who has contrivance enough to get himself into a jail; for, being in a ship is being in a jail, with the chance of being drowned. . . . The man in a jail has more room, better food, and commonly better company, and is in safety." 🔖

tatterdemálion [*tatter* and I know not what.] A ragged fellow.

teague A name of contempt used for an Irishman.

❦ Although Boswell several times suggested they make a tour to Ireland, Johnson wasn't interested: "It is the last place where I should wish to travel." Boswell ran through the usual list of attractions. Dublin? "No, Sir; Dublin is only a worse capital." What about the otherworldly volcanic landscape in the north of Ireland called the Giant's Causeway—was that worth seeing? "Worth seeing, yes; but not worth going to see." Still, he liked the Irish, not least because in his estimation they weren't as self-satisfied as the Scots. "The Irish," he said, "are not a conspiracy to cheat the world by false representations of the merits of their countrymen. No, Sir; the Irish are a FAIR PEOPLE;—they never speak well of one another." 🔖

térmagant A scold; a brawling turbulent woman. It appears in Shakespeare to have been anciently used of men.

I could have such a fellow whipt for o'erdoing termagant; it outherod's Herod. Shakespeare's Hamlet.

She threw his periwig into the fire; well, said he, thou art a brave termagant. Tatler, N° 54.

thíck-sculled Dull; stupid.

This downright fighting fool, this thick-scull'd hero,
This blunt unthinking instrument of death,
With plain dull virtue has outgone my wit. Dryden.

thickskin [*thick* and *skin.*] A coarse gross man; a numskul.

thrasónical [from *Thraso*, a boaster in old comedy.] Boastful; bragging.

> *There never was any thing so sudden but the fight of two rams, and Cae-*
> *sar's thrasonical brag of, I came, saw, and overcame.* Shakesp. As you
> like it.

> ❦ *Thrasonical* comes from Thraso, a character in Terence's play *The*
> *Eunuch.* ❧

thréepenny [*triobolaris*, Lat.] Vulgar; mean.

tillyfally, tíllyvalley A word used formerly when any thing said was
rejected as trifling or impertinent.

> *Tillyfally, sir John, never tell me; your ancient swaggerer comes not in my*
> *doors.* Shakesp. Henry IV. p. ii.

> ❦ Not properly an insult, but a fine word to have in any verbal arsenal.
> It means something like "Nonsense!" or "Pish-tosh!" Whether John-
> son ever used the word is unclear; his favorite equivalent was "Pho!" or
> "Poh, poh!" He once cut Frances Burney off with "Pho! fiddle-faddle!"
> Late in his life, two ladies visited him and "repeated a speech of some
> length, previously prepared for the occasion. It was an enthusiastic ef-
> fusion, which, when the speaker had finished, she panted for her idol's
> reply." Johnson's answer was brief: "Fiddle-de-dee, my dear." ❧

típpler [from *tipple.*] A sottish drunkard; an idle drunken fellow.

tit

* A small horse: generally in contempt.
* A woman: in contempt.

tómboy [*Tom* a diminutive of *Thomas*, and *boy.*] A mean fellow; some-times a wild coarse girl.

tóper [from *tope.*] A drunkard.

❦ As a young man, Johnson boasted of being able to hold his liquor: He once drank "three bottles of port without being the worse for it." Wine was kids' stuff: "Claret is the liquor for boys; port, for men; but he who aspires to be a hero must drink brandy. . . . Brandy will do soonest for a man what drinking *can* do for him."

But in later life he refused to drink at all because, said Boswell, "he could not do it in moderation." And so he became what the eigh-teenth century called a "water-drinker," which struck contempo-raries as eccentric. (Before the days of water purification, alcohol was safer because it killed bacteria.) A lady who wouldn't believe he was really a teetotaler insisted, "I am sure, sir, you would not carry it too far." But Johnson was sincere: "Nay, madam, it carried me."

He therefore derided those who drank too heavily. His friend Christopher Smart—"poor Kit Smart"—was confined to a hospital, and someone lamented that he'd no longer get any exercise. "Exer-cise!" said Johnson. "I never heard that he used any: he might, for aught I know, walk *to* the alehouse; but I believe he was always *car-ried* home again." And of one lush, he had only this to say: "The difference between that woman when alive, and when she shall be dead, is only this. When alive she calls for beer. When dead she'll call for beer no longer."

tósspot [*toss* and *pot.*] A toper and drunkard.

trífler [*trifelaar*, Dutch.] One who acts with levity; one that talks with folly.

trióbolar [*triobolaris*, Latin.] Vile; mean; worthless.

Turn your libel into verse, and then it may pass current amongst the balladmongers for a triobolar ballad. Cheynel.

The Latin *triobolaris* means "worth three obols," a Greek coin worth just one-sixth of a drachm. So *triobolar* is just a fancy equivalent of *threepenny*.

tróllop [A low word, I know not whence derived.] A slatternly, loose woman.

trúbtail A short squat woman. Ainsworth.

trull [*trulla*, Italian.] A low whore; a vagrant strumpet.

In a note on Shakespeare's *Antony and Cleopatra*, Johnson commented on the history of this word: "It may be observed, that 'trull' was not, in our authour's time, a term of mere infamy, but a word of slight contempt, as 'wench' is now."

tun [*tunne*, Sax. *tonne*, Dut. *tonne*, *tonneau*, Fr.]

+ A large cask.

+ A drunkard. In burlesque.

Here's a tun of midnight—work to come,
Og from a treason-tavern rolling home. Dryden.

U

úgly [This word was antiently written *ougly;* whence Mr. Dier ingeniously deduces it from *ouphlike;* that is, like an *ouph*, *elf*, or *goblin*. In Saxon *oga* is terrour; and in Gothic *ogan* is to fear.] Deformed; offensive to the sight; contrary to beautiful.

❦When people praised some woman as "very beautiful," Johnson would have none of it: "She was as bad as negative badness could be, and stood in the way of what was good. . . . Such a woman might be cut out of a cabbage by a skilful artificer." But he could be just as harsh about himself. Johnson was terribly ugly: He was tall and gangly, and a childhood case of scrofula left his face disfigured. Hester Thrale noted, "Fear was I believe the first emotion in the hearts of all his beholders"; even his wife, Tetty, found his appearance "very forbidding" and "hideously striking to the eye" at first sight. While Frances Burney examined a protrait of Johnson, he looked over her shoulder and "began see-sawing for a moment or two in silence." He then burst out, "Ah ha!—Sam Johnson!—I see thee!—and an ugly dog thou art!"❦

underféllow [*under* and *fellow.*] A mean man; a sorry wretch.

uxórious [*uxorius*, Lat.] Submissively fond of a wife; infected with connubial dotage.

> *How would'st thou insult,*
> *When I must live uxorious to thy will*
> *In perfect thraldom, how again betray me?* Milton.

V

váuntful [*vaunt* and *full.*] Boastful; ostentatious.

venditátion [*venditatio*, from *vendito*, Latin.] Boastful display.

víled [from *vile*, whence *revile.*] Abusive; scurrilous; defamatory.

> *He granted life to all except to me, who had used vil'd speeches against king Edward.* Hayward.

víllain [*vilain*, Fr. *villanus*, low Latin.] A wicked wretch.

> *O villain! villain! his very opinion in the letter. Abhorred villain! unnatural, detested, brutish villain!* Shakesp.

❧ The history of the word *villain* is dripping with class prejudice. It comes from the Latin *villa*, "a country estate." In the feudal system of the Middle Ages, a *villain* or *villein* was a serf entirely subject to the lord whose land he worked. From "low-born rustic" the term came to mean "one lacking in good breeding" (or *courtesy*, which would be learned in the *court*), and from there to "a criminal."

virágo [Latin.]

- A female warriour; a woman with the qualities of a man.
- It is commonly used in detestation for an impudent turbulent woman.

Perhaps Johnson's most famous insult comes from Boswell. The two went to a Quaker meeting. Unlike the Anglicans, the Quakers allowed women preachers. According to Boswell, Johnson observed, "Sir, a woman's preaching is like a dog's walking on his hinder legs. It is not done well; but you are surprized to find it done at all."

People have assumed ever since that Johnson was a bitter misogynist, and stories circulated by others haven't helped his reputation. William Seward, for instance, tells the story that a "very talkative lady" didn't take the hint when Johnson tried repeatedly to ignore her. Finally, she said, "Why, Doctor, I believe you prefer the company of men to that of the ladies." "Madam," said Johnson, "I am very fond of the company of ladies; I like their beauty, I like their delicacy, I like their vivacity, and I like their *silence*." But the image of Johnson as a mean-spirited male chauvinist is undeserved. Yes, he scolded a friend for spending his time "with a set of wretched *un-idea'd* girls," but this doesn't mean he thought all women un-idea'd. As his friend Frances Reynolds observed, "Johnson set a higher value upon female friendship than, perhaps, most men."

W

wag [*wagian*, Saxon, to cheat.] Any one ludicrously mischievous; a merry droll.

We wink at wags, when they offend,
And spare the boy, in hopes the man may mend. Dryden.

❧ Johnson once told Frances Burney, "Every man has some time in his life, an ambition to be a wag." ❧

wántwit [*want* and *wit.*] A fool; an idiot.

Such a wantwit sadness makes of me,
That I have much ado to know myself. Shakespeare.

❧ As the compiler of *Dr. Johnson's Table Talk* tells the story, a "very ignorant man" once burst out laughing at something Johnson had said. "Pray, Sir," asked Johnson, "what does that man laugh at? I hope I have said nothing that he could possibly understand." ❧

wássailer [from *wassail.*] A toper; a drunkard.

I'm loth to meet the rudeness, and swill'd insolence
Of such late wassailers. Milton.

❧ Johnson loved twitting the hard-drinking Boswell, who often recounted his hangovers after long nights of boozing. Johnson corrected him: "Nay, Sir, it was not the *wine* that made your head ache, but the *sense* that I put into it." Boswell suggested at least this advantage: "Drinking drives away care, and makes us forget whatever is disagreeable. Would not you allow a man to drink for that reason?" Johnson quipped, "Yes, Sir, if he sat next *you*."

After a night of carousing in the Scottish islands, Boswell "awaked at noon, with a severe head-ach." He lay in bed, awaiting the inevitable dressing-down from the great sage. But Johnson was in a good mood, and around one o'clock came into Boswell's room and teased him out of bed: "What, drunk yet?" Boswell feebly tried to justify himself: "Sir, they kept me up." "No," Johnson insisted, "you kept them up, you drunken dog!" Boswell was relieved by his "good-humoured *English* pleasantry."

whelp [*welp*, Dutch; *huolpar*, Islandick; *hwalp*, Swedish.]

+ The young of a dog; a puppy.

+ A young man. In contempt.

That aukward whelp, with his money-bags, would have made his entrance. Addison's Guardian.

w h e l p

Whig [hwœg, Saxon.] The name of a faction.

If there was any group Johnson enjoyed taunting more than the Scots, it was the Whigs, one of the main political parties of the day. Johnson was widely known as a Tory, and he used his *Dictionary* to point up the differences between them: A Tory is "one who adheres to the antient constitution of the state, and the apostolical hierarchy of the church of England"; a Whig is merely "the name of a faction."

"Every bad man," he lectured Boswell, "is a Whig," and "the first

Whig was the Devil." He once gave this advice to a young man: "I have seen a great deal of the world, and take it upon my word and experience, that where you see a Whig you see a rascal." The politician William Pulteney, for instance, was "as paltry a fellow as could be." His crime? "He was a Whig, who pretended to be honest; and you know it is ridiculous for a Whig to pretend to be honest."

Johnson, said Hester Thrale, "not only loved a tory himself, but he loved a man the better if he heard he hated a whig." He described one friend as "a man to my very heart's content: he hated a fool, and he hated a rogue, and he hated a *whig*; he was a very good *hater*."

whore [*hor*, Saxon; *hoere*, Dutch.]

- A woman who converses unlawfully with men; a fornicatress; an adultress; a strumpet.

- A prostitute; a woman who receives men for money.

On matters of sexual morality, Johnson could be unforgiving. Boswell argued that a woman whose husband had been unfaithful should be able to "indulge herself in gallantries [affairs] with equal freedom as her husband does." Johnson was not amused. "This lady of yours, Sir, I think, is very fit for a brothel."

Real prostitutes, though, like all disadvantaged people, earned not Johnson's scorn but his pity. Johnson's friend George Steevens wrote that "among his singularities, his love of conversing with the prostitutes whom he met with in the streets was not the least." He'd sit with them in taverns, "striving to awaken in them a proper sense of their condition." Friends teased him, saying his real intentions weren't quite so moral; but he'd answer, "No Sir; we never proceeded to the *Opus Magnum*." When Johnson asked one prostitute "for what purpose she supposed her Maker had bestowed on her so much beauty," she answered, "To please the gentlemen, to be sure; for what other use could it be given me?" He was genuinely saddened by the loss of human potential. 📖

whoremáster, whoremónger [*whore* and *master* or *monger*.] One who keeps whores, or converses with a fornicatress.

What is a whoremaster, fool? a fool in good cloaths and something like thee. Shakespeare.

whóreson [*whore* and *son*.] A bastard. It is generally used in a ludicrous dislike.

Thou whoreson Zed! though unnecessary letter. Shakespeare.

❧ Johnson mulled over Kent's strange insult in *King Lear*—why was *zed* (the British name for the letter *z*) an "unnecessary letter"? In his edition of the play, Johnson added a footnote: "I do not well understand how a man is reproached by being called *Zed*, nor how Z is an *unnecessary letter*. . . . Perhaps it was written thou *whoreson* C (for *cuckold*) *thou unnecessary letter*. C is a letter unnecessary in our alphabet, one of its two sounds being represented by S, and one by K." 📖

wiseácre [It was antiently written *wisesegger*, as the Dutch *wiseggher*, a soothsayer.]

- A wise, or sententious man. Obsolete.
- A fool; a dunce.

Why, says a wiseacre that sat by him, were I as the king of France, I would scorn to take part with footmen. Addison.

witling [Diminutive of *wit*.] A pretender to wit; a man of petty smartness.

Those half-learn'd witlings num'rous in our isle,
As half-form'd insects on the banks of Nile. Pope.

❦Johnson could be stinging when witlings got on his nerves. An early biographer reported on "one of Dr. Johnson's rudest speeches," when "a pompous gentleman" met him in Lichfield and vapidly said, "Dr. Johnson, we have had a most excellent discourse to-day!" "That may be," said Johnson; "but, it is impossible that you should know it." Perhaps Johnson's young friend Frances Burney had people like this in mind when she wrote a play called *The Witlings.*❧

wittol [*wittol*, Sax.] A man who knows the falsehood of his wife and seems contented; a tame cuckold.

❦An irritating "young gentleman" once asked, "Would you advise me to marry?" Johnson, thinking his question was posed "disrespectfully," answered angrily. "I would advise no man to marry, Sir, who is not likely to propagate understanding." As for second marriages: "The triumph of hope over experience."❧

witworm [*wit* and *worm*.] One that feeds on wit; a canker of wit.

Z

zány [Probably of *zanei*. The contraction of *Giovanni* or *sanna*, a scoff, according to Skinner.] One employed to raise laughter by his gestures, actions and speeches; a merry Andrew; a buffoon.

> *Some carrytale, some pleaseman, some slight zany,*
> *Some mumblenews, some trencher knight, some Dick,*
> *Told our intents before.* Shakespeare.

> *Oh, great restorer of the good old stage,*
> *Preacher at once, and zany of thy age.* Pope's Dunciad.

ACKNOWLEDGMENTS

In a book of insults, where every sentence is buzzing with malice or dripping with venom, it's a pleasure to take one page to express some sincere appreciation.

Johnson had a sharp tongue but he was no ingrate, and he offered well-turned compliments when they were deserved. "The booksellers," he said of his publishers, "are generous liberal-minded men." My own publishers are just as generous and liberal-minded men—and women. Thanks go first to Mim Harrison at Levenger Press, whose championship of *Samuel Johnson's Dictionary* begat this mischievous offspring. Steve and Lori Leveen of Levenger and George Gibson and his crew at Walker have all been wonderfully supportive.

I'm especially grateful to Frank Lynch (no relation), whose delightful and well-organized collection of Johnsoniana was my starting point in this book.

My colleagues and students at Rutgers University in Newark, New Jersey, offered some handy advice. As always, the staffs at Rutgers University Libraries and Princeton University Library made my work easy.

Finally, I thank my wife, Laura, who is slowly becoming a Johnsonian against her will.

BIBLIOGRAPHY

The American Heritage Dictionary. 4th ed. Boston: Houghton Mifflin, 2000.

Bierce, Ambrose. *The Devil's Dictionary.* Ed. Roy Morris. Oxford: Oxford University Press, 1999.

Boswell, James. *Boswell's Journal of a Tour to the Hebrides with Samuel Johnson, LL.D., Now First Published from the Original Manuscript.* Ed. Frederick A. Pottle and Charles H. Bennett. London: William Heinemann, 1936.

————. *The Life of Samuel Johnson.* Ed. G. B. Hill, rev. L. F. Powell. 6 vols. Oxford: Clarendon Press, 1934–64.

Burney, Fanny. *Dr Johnson & Fanny Burney: Being the Johnsonian Passages from the Works of Mme. D'Arblay.* Ed. Chauncey Brewster Tinker. New York: Moffat, Yard, 1911.

Cooper, Lane. "Dr. Johnson on Oats and Other Grains." *PMLA* 52 (September 1937): 785–802.

Curley, Thomas M. "Johnson and America." *The Age of Johnson: A Scholarly Annual* 6 (1994): 31–73.

Dr. Johnson's Table-Talk: Containing Aphorisms on Literature, Life, and Manners, with Anecdotes of Distinguished Persons. London, 1798.

Farmer, J. S., and W. E. Henley. *Historical Dictionary of Slang: An Alphabetical History of Colloquial, Unorthodox, Underground and Vulgar English.* 2 vols. Ware, Hertfordshire: Wordsworth Editions, 1987.

Grose, Francis. *The Canting Academy . . . Also a Compleat Canting Dictionary, Both of Old Words, and Such as Are Now Most in Use: A Book Very Useful and Necessary (to Be Known, but Not Practised) for All People.* 2nd ed. London, 1788.

———. *Lexicon Balatronicum: A Dictionary of Buckish Slang, University Wit, and Pickpocket Eloquence.* London, 1811.

Hawkins, Sir John. *The Life of Samuel Johnson.* Vol. 1 of *The Works of Samuel Johnson.* London, 1787.

Hill, G. B., ed. *Johnsonian Miscellanies.* 2 vols. Oxford: Clarendon Press, 1897.

Johnson, Samuel. *A Dictionary of the English Language.* 2 vols. London, 1755.

———. *The Letters of Samuel Johnson.* Ed. Bruce Redford. 5 vols. Princeton: Princeton University Press, 1992–94.

———. *Lives of the English Poets.* Ed. G. B. Hill. 3 vols. Oxford: Clarendon Press, 1905.

———. *The Yale Edition of the Works of Samuel Johnson.* 13 vols. to date. New Haven: Yale University Press, 1958– .

Johnsoniana; or, A Collection of Bon Mots, &c. Dublin, 1776.

Lynch, Frank. "The Samuel Johnson Sound-Bite Page." http://www.samueljohnson.com.

Lynch, Jack. "Lord Mayor Wilkes, Liberty, & No. 45." *Colonial Williamsburg: The Journal of the Colonial Williamsburg Foundation* 25, no. 2 (Summer 2003): 51–55.

The Oxford English Dictionary. 2nd ed. 20 vols. Oxford: Oxford University Press, 1989.

Partridge, Eric. *A Dictionary of Slang and Unconventional English: Colloquialisms and Catch-Phrases, Solecisms and Catachreses, Nicknames, Vulgarisms and Such Americanisms as Have Been Naturalized.* 7th ed. New York: Macmillan, 1970.

Piozzi, Hester Lynch. *Thraliana: The Diary of Mrs. Hester Lynch Thrale (Later Mrs. Piozzi).* Ed. Katharine C. Balderston. 2 vols. Oxford: Clarendon Press, 1942.

Read, Allen Walker. "The History of Dr. Johnson's Definition of *Oats.*" *Agricultural History* 8 (July 1934): 81–94.

Rogers, Pat. *The Samuel Johnson Encyclopedia.* Westport, Conn.: Greenwood Press, 1996.

Shakespeare, William. *The Works of William Shakespeare.* Ed. Samuel Johnson. 8 vols. London, 1765.

Sledd, James H., and Gwin J. Kolb. "Johnson's Definitions of *Whig* and *Tory.*" *PMLA* 67 (September 1952): 882–85.

Tyson, Moses, and Henry Guppy. *The French Journals of Mrs. Thrale and Doctor Johnson.* New York: Haskell House, 1973.

Wimsatt, W. K. "Johnson and Scots." *Times Literary Supplement* (March 9, 1946): 115.

Winokur, Jon. *The Portable Curmudgeon.* New York: New American Library, 1987.

INDEX OF SELECTED
PERSONAGES

BIRCH, THOMAS (1705–66), clergyman and biographer, and one of the first friends Johnson made after arriving in London. See **dull**

BLAIR, HUGH (1718–1800), Scottish clergyman and critic; defender of the authenticity of Ossian's poetry. See **ruffian**

BOSWELL, JAMES (1740–95), Scottish lawyer and biographer of Johnson. See **backfriend**, **bedlam**, **bellygod**, **blockhead**, **booby**, **cant**, **cracker**, **dull**, **dupe**, **enthusiast**, **fatwitted**, **jack pudding**, **malapert**, **manhater**, **merry-andrew**, **mouth-friend**, **noier**, **nonsense**, **oats**, **patriot**, **pension**, **pettifogger**, *poetaster*, **politicaster**, **rascal**, **republican**, **scelerat**, **scoundrel**, **stateswoman**, **tarpawling**, **teague**, **toper**, *virago*, **wassailer**, **Whig**, **whore**

BURNEY, FRANCES (FANNY) (1752–1840), writer known for her diaries and for her novels, *Evelina*, *Cecilia*, *Camilla*, and *The Wanderer*. See **baggage**, **flasher**, **plaguy**, **tillyfally**, **ugly**, **wag**, **witling**

CHESTERFIELD, PHILIP DORMER STANHOPE, FOURTH EARL OF (1694–1773), politician and would-be patron of Johnson's *Dictionary*. See **dupe**, **patron**, **ruffian**

CHEYNE, GEORGE (1671–1743), medical writer. See *scelerat*

CHURCHILL, CHARLES (1731–64), satirical poet who ridiculed Johnson. See **pension**, *poetaster*

DAVIES, THOMAS (c. 1712–85), bookseller and owner of the shop where Boswell and Johnson first met. *See* **oats**

DERRICK, SAMUEL (1724–69), Irish miscellaneous writer. *See* **rhymer**

EDWARDS, THOMAS (1699–1757), critic and poet. *See* **bookworm**

FIELDING, HENRY (1707–54), playwright and novelist, best known for *Joseph Andrews* and *Tom Jones*. *See* **scribbler**

FOOTE, SAMUEL (1720–77), playwright and actor. *See* **half-scholar**

GARRICK, DAVID (1717–79), the most famous actor of the eighteenth century and Johnson's one-time student in Lichfield. *See* **doxy, jack pudding, merry-andrew**

GAY, JOHN (1685–1732), poet and playwright, best known for *The Beggar's Opera*; Johnson wrote his *Life*. *See* **plaguy**

GOLDSMITH, OLIVER (c. 1728–74), Irish writer, best known for *The Vicar of Wakefield* and *She Stoops to Conquer*. *See* **dull, fatwitted, plaguy**

GRAINGER, JAMES (c. 1723–67), Scottish poet, best known for *The Sugar Cane*. *See* **poetaster**

GRAY, THOMAS (1716–71), poet, best known for "An Elegy Written in a Country Church-Yard." *See* **dull**

HARRIS, JAMES (1709–80), critic and philosopher, known as "Hermes Harris" after his treatise on language, *Hermes*. *See* **grammaticáster**

HAWKINS, SIR JOHN (1719–89), lawyer and author; friend to and biographer of Johnson. *See* **inconversable**

JOHNSON, ELIZABETH (TETTY) (1689–1752), Johnson's wife. *See* **ugly**

KNOWLES, MARY (1733–1807), friend of Johnson, called the "ingenious Quaker lady." *See* **prig**

LONG, DUDLEY (1748–1829), Whig politician. *See* **punster**

RAYNAL, GUILLAUME-THOMAS (1713–96), French philosopher and historian, dismissed from the priesthood. *See* **sabbathbreaker**

REYNOLDS, FRANCES (1729–1807), artist and sister of Sir Joshua Reynolds. *See* *virago*

REYNOLDS, SIR JOSHUA (1723–92), the most important painter and critic of late eighteenth-century England. *See* **coxcomical, jack pudding, scribbler**

ROUSSEAU, JEAN-JACQUES (1712–78), Swiss author and philosopher. *See* **nonsense**

SEWARD, WILLIAM (1744–99), writer and scientist. *See* *virago*

SHAKESPEARE, WILLIAM (1564–1616), playwright; Johnson edited his *Works*. *See* **cuckoldmaker, scribbler**

SHERIDAN, RICHARD BRINSLEY (1751–1816), politician and playwright, best known for *The School for Scandal*. *See* **plaguy**

SHERIDAN, THOMAS (1719–88), actor and father of Richard Brinsley Sheridan. *See* **dull**

SMART, CHRISTOPHER (1722–71), poet. *See* **rhymer, toper**

SMITH, ADAM (1723–90), Scottish economist and philosopher, best known for *The Wealth of Nations*. *See* **stockjobber**

STEEVENS, GEORGE (1736–1800), scholar and reviser of Johnson's Shakespeare edition. *See* **whore**

STERNE, LAURENCE (1713–68), Irish clergyman and novelist, best known for *Tristram Shandy*. *See* **dunce**

SWIFT, JONATHAN (1667–1745), Irish clergyman and writer, best known for *Gulliver's Travels*; Johnson wrote his *Life*. *See* **dunce, garlickeater, scribbler**

THOMSON, JAMES (1700–1748), Scottish poet, best known for *The Seasons*. *See* **fustian**

THRALE, HESTER (1741–1821), one of Johnson's closest friends and author of an early Johnson biography. *See* **backfriend, bellygod, blockhead, cant, cotquean, flasher, giddybrained, to gloze, grumbler, oats, plaguy, punster, tarpawling, ugly, Whig**

THRALE, HESTER MARIA (QUEENEY) (1764–1857), daughter of Henry and Hester Thrale, nicknamed Queeney by Johnson. *See* **giddybrained, tarpawling**

WALPOLE, HORACE, FOURTH EARL OF ORFORD (1717–97), author and collector, best known for his Gothic novel *The Castle of Otranto* and his voluminous correspondence. *See* **crabbed, nincompoop**

WARBURTON, WILLIAM (1698–1779), clergyman and editor of Shakespeare's *Works*. See **bookworm**

WOLCOT, JOHN (1738–1819), satirical poet who wrote under the pseudonym Peter Pindar. *See* **cracker**

YOUNG, EDWARD (1683–1765), clergyman and poet, best known for *Night Thoughts*. *See* **poetaster**

Feeding the Mind
BY LEWIS CARROLL

A Fortnight in the Wilderness
BY ALEXIS DE TOCQUEVILLE

Painting as a Pastime
BY WINSTON S. CHURCHILL

Rare Words
and ways to master their meanings
BY JAN LEIGHTON AND HALLIE LEIGHTON

The Silverado Squatters
Six selected chapters
BY ROBERT LOUIS STEVENSON

Sir Winston Churchill's Life Through His Paintings
BY DAVID COOMBS WITH MINNIE CHURCHILL
FOREWORD BY MARY SOAMES

Words That Make a Difference
and how to use them in a masterly way
BY ROBERT GREENMAN